BLACK ✦ STARS

AFRICAN AMERICAN WOMEN SCIENTISTS AND INVENTORS

✦

OTHA RICHARD SULLIVAN, ED.D.

JIM HASKINS, GENERAL EDITOR

John Wiley & Sons, Inc.

Copyright © 2002 by Otha Sullivan. All rights reserved
Foreword copyright © 2002 by Georgia Williams Scaife, Ph.D.

Published by John Wiley & Sons, Inc., New York
Published simultaneously in Canada

Design and production by Navta Associates, Inc.

Library of Congress Cataloging-in-Publication Data:

Sullivan, Otha Richard
    Black stars : African American women scientists and inventors / Otha Richard Sullivan;
    Jim Haskins, general editor.
       p.   cm. — (Black stars)
    Includes bibliographical references.
    ISBN 0-471-38707-X (cloth : alk. paper)
       1. Afro-American inventors—Biography.   2. Afro-American scientists—Biography.
   3. Afro-American women.   [1. Inventors—Biography.   2. Afro-Americans—Biography.]
   I. Haskins, James, 1941-   II. Title.   III. Black stars (New York, N.Y.)

T39 .S985   2001
608.9'96'073—dc21
[B]   2001017924

Printed in the United States of America
10 9 8 7 6 5 4 3 2 1

Dedicated to Dewitt Sullivan, CPA,
My Brother and Mentor

CONTENTS

FOREWORD

It's about time! *African American Women Scientists and Inventors* by Dr. Otha Sullivan could not have been written at a more critical time. At the dawn of the twenty-first century, we stand, again, at the crossroads with racism, race relations, and discrimination in our country. There is much talk about reparations, affirmative action, achievement gaps, and many other issues seething with racial overtones. Solutions to our racial problems seem to escape even the most brilliant among us.

A keen awareness of one's history and self pride may be the most critical answer to the problems. A wonderful start is with the African American woman and her role in science and inventions. Dr. Sullivan could have written about her role in education, art, literature, music, or dance. He would have found much more historical documentation in these more traditional areas. Even today, and among nonminority women especially, science and inventions are considered nontraditional pursuits for women. Perhaps, he wanted more of a challenge. Or perhaps he is writing with one purpose of truly jolting our self pride and respect for our history. Indeed, he achieves this with *African American Women Scientists and Inventors.*

What Dr. Sullivan does in writing about such inventions as the folding cabinet-bed by Sara E. Goode and the scientific work on sickle cell anemia by Dr. Angela D. Ferguson is to take us by surprise! Who would have thought that in the midst of social and economic barriers, racism, and discrimination, the creativity of these women would thrive and emerge. Is there a message here for today's students who are often told that boys are better suited to subjects like technology and science? Is there a message here for the poor African American—boy or girl—that says, if amazing things could happen after the Civil War and in the midst of the Emancipation Proclamation, if women could make these contributions and persevere in the face of such barriers, could amazing things possibly happen for me?

Dr. Sullivan has done more than dig deeply and unveil almost untold stories about great African American women scientists and inventors. What he has done is to provide hope for the millions of African American girls and boys who have lost hope because they never see anyone "like me." He has given them role models to read about and to emulate. He has also taught us that if you look hard enough and with resiliency, the truth can be found and told. I hope that teachers will embrace *African American Women Scientists and Inventors* and use it to find some solutions to discrimination, racism, and achievement gaps based on color that continue to plague our classrooms and society.

Georgia Williams Scaife, Ph.D.
U.S. Department of Defense
Education Activity

ACKNOWLEDGMENTS

A special thanks to Stedman Mays, my literary agent at Clausen, Mays and Tahan, for his support in the development of this project and efforts in finding a home for this book.

Thanks to my brother, Dewitt Sullivan, for being that special role model in my life. To my sister, Donnie, and brothers, Joseph Benjamin and Lemon, for your unconditional support.

Thanks to all of my inquisitive students in Detroit, Washington, D.C., Highland Park, Michigan, and Lorman, Mississippi, over the past thirty years. Dr. Betty Nyangoni and Dr. Georgia Williams encouraged me to write over the years. Andrew "Rudy" Rudolph and Betty Colden, who have passed on, still watch over me and give me strength and determination to share the contributions of our people. Wonderful African American women scientists and inventors provided interviews, information, and suggestions in this effort. Dr. Josephine M. Posey, dean of education and psychology at Alcorn State University, provided support and assistance as developmental editor.

Carole Hall, my editor at John Wiley & Sons, believed in this project and made numerous helpful suggestions. Carrette Perkins and Camille Acker also contributed to the editing and photo research, keeping me on task. Associate managing editor, Kimberly Monroe, and copyeditor, Mary Dorian, added their expertise. Jim Haskins accepted this work in the Black Stars biography series. I am grateful to each of these individuals for their support.

INTRODUCTION

✦

Throughout history, women scientists and inventors have made fascinating discoveries and created many useful tools. But a search in libraries throughout the world reveals little information about these contributions.

We will probably never know the extent to which African American women contributed to science and invention due to the social and economic barriers they faced. Today we know that countless enslaved African American women were inventors but could not receive patents. Why? Prior to 1865, it was unlawful to issue patents to slaves. Only the slave owner could receive a patent.

After the Civil War and the Emancipation Proclamation, African American inventors could apply for and receive patents for their inventions. But African American women still did not get the credit they deserved. Many of their inventions were recorded under the names of their fathers, husbands, brothers, and other males.

In the early decades of the twentieth century, women were denied equal opportunities in education and employment, and they were not allowed to vote. Still denied credit or little known for their discoveries and inventions, African American women continued to bring their talents to science and technology.

Like other inventive women across history, the early black women discoverers and inventors commonly used their talents in the home. Creativity and ingenuity are evident in Sara E. Goode's invention of the folding cabinet-bed, Alice H. Parker's improvement on a heating furnace, and later, in Marie Van Brittan Brown's invention of a video and audio home security system.

Outside the home in industry, health, space, and the military, African American women have also made valuable advancements. These contributions include the test for explosives by chemist and inventor Betty Harris, Ph.D.; sickle cell anemia research by Angela Ferguson, M.D.; and the cancer research of Jane Cooke Wright, M.D. Although African Americans today make up only 4.5 percent of all science and engineering professionals, many women can be counted among them.

Too often, the contributions of all women in science and invention—regardless of color—are still unsung. Consequently, many girls mistakenly believe that careers in science and technology are not for them. Women have indeed achieved success and prominence in these fields through their ideas, discoveries and inventions. This book is an attempt to fill a void in the pages of American history by introducing some of their stories to you. The stars of these stories are as diverse as they are talented. Some are loners and fiercely independent. Others enjoy collaborating with others in teams in major universities or corporations. Some of the women are famous and others are little known outside their field of endeavor. But each was determined to make her vision a reality.

This book, like its companion volume, *African American Inventors,* and other titles in the Black Stars biography series, invites students, teachers, and people of all colors everywhere to encourage youth and their potential. Use it to teach discipline, develop character, and instill pride, self-esteem, and know-how. Use it to prove the worth of problem-solving skills and to ignite the imagination and an interest in mathematics and science, the keys to invention.

PART ONE

◆

THE
EARLY YEARS

E L L E N F.
EGLIN

(1 8 4 9 – ?)

✦

Ellen F. Eglin of Washington, D.C., was one of the ingenious early African American women inventors who made her living as a housekeeper. She invented a special type of clothes-wringer in the 1880s. She might have made a fortune from her mechanical talent. But Eglin settled for a few dollars, believing that she would not be able to find a manufacturer to produce her invention. She sold it for the meager sum of $18 to a white person interested in manufacturing the product. The buyer reaped considerable financial rewards.

Always practical, Eglin shrugged off her disappointment. In the April 1890 issue of *Woman Inventor,* the first publication about women inventors in the United States or Europe, she gave her reasons for selling her invention:

> You know I am black and if it was known that a Negro woman patented the invention, white ladies would not buy the wringer. I was afraid to be known because of my color in having it introduced into the market, that is the only reason.[1]

In fact, few early African American scientists and inventors were known at all. For centuries, ingenious black men and women in America, like their African ancestors, had been inventing and discovering new and useful things. For example, before the Revolutionary war, Onesimus, a slave in Massachusetts in 1706, is credited with discovering a remedy for smallpox. Benjamin Banneker, born free in Maryland in 1731, measured the movement of the stars and accurately predicted a solar eclipse.

THE SPIRIT OF INVENTION

Benjamin **Banneker** (1731–1806) had extraordinary mechanical gifts. For example, as a youth he spent many hours and weeks disassembling and putting a pocket watch back together again.

While working on the watch, Banneker must have mused, "Why not make one!" He seized on the idea, perhaps not even knowing that no one else in North America had ever made a clock. Peter Heinrich, his Quaker teacher, mentor, and friend, gave him a few items that he thought might help—a journal from London with a picture of a clock, a geometry book, and a book about the laws of motion.

Banneker studied the books, and, using an old compass and a ruler for measurements, began making the intricate calculations necessary to design the gears. Carefully carving each gear by hand out of wood, Banneker finished his clock two years later in 1753. It kept perfect time for more than forty years, striking every hour. People came from all over the countryside to see it and to meet its creator. Banneker was only twenty-two years old when he made the clock.

◆ Isaac Newton's three **laws of motion** explained why and how things move. Newton, an English scientist, lived from 1642 to 1727.

◆ **Calculations** are the steps in working out math problems.

By the 1790s, there were 697,624 people of African descent in the new United States. Some, like Banneker, had been born free; others had earned their freedom fighting in the Revolutionary War; and still others had bought freedom for themselves and their families. Free blacks could be awarded patents for their inventions. For example, Norbert Rillieux, born free in New Orleans in 1806, secured patents on his inventions using a steam engine to refine sugar. Rillieux's inventions took the sugar industry by storm.

In contrast to Norbert Rillieux, enslaved inventors got no recognition or protection for their great ideas. Hezekiah, an Alabama slave, invented a cotton-cleaning machine around 1825. Joe Anderson, Cyrus McCormick's enslaved assistant, inspired the invention of the harvester. But because Hezekiah and Joe Anderson were among the 90 percent of African Americans held captive until President Lincoln issued the Emancipation Proclamation in 1863, neither could receive patents on their inventions.

Neither could the slaves belonging to Eli Whitney, who are credited with giving him the idea for a comblike device to clean cotton. That device, the cotton gin, revolutionized the economy of the entire South.

In 1913, Henry E. Baker of the United States Patent Office compiled four volumes of patent drawings for inventions primarily by black men. Entitled *The Colored Inventor,* Baker's collection listed some 1,200 inventions.

Baker discovered in his research that some black inventors did not want others to know they were African American. He wrote:

> Sometimes it has been difficult to get this information by correspondence even from colored inventors themselves. Many of them refuse to acknowledge that their inventions are in any way identified with the colored race, on the ground, presumably, that the publication of that fact might adversely affect

the commercial value of their invention; and in view of the prevailing sentiment in many sections of our country, it cannot be denied that much reason lies at the bottom of such conclusion.[2]

While Eglin sold her clothes-wringer, she continued to work on another device. She was hopeful that she would patent this invention. She explained in *Woman Inventor:*

> I am working on another invention and have money to push it after the patent is issued to me, and the invention will be known as a black woman's. I am looking forward to exhibiting the model at the Woman's International Industrial Inventors Congress to which women are invited to participate regardless of color lines.

The publisher of *Woman Inventor* befriended Eglin and sought to help her patent her invention. Eglin attended a reception given by President William Henry Harrison for inventors. She later worked as a clerk in the census office. But there is no evidence that she patented her second invention, and what it was remains unknown. Fortunately, many other black women patented their innovations, so their story can be told.

GENIUS IN THE HOUSE

SARAH BOONE

Sarah Boone received a patent for her improvement on the ironing board in 1892. It was a special sleeve-ironing board, adapted for pressing the inside and outside of coat sleeves. It was also convenient in pressing curved-waist seams on ladies' and men's garments.

◆ A **patent** is legal proof that a certain person created an invention so that others cannot claim that they produced the item first.

JUDY W. REED

Judy W. Reed patented an improvement for a dough kneader and roller on September 20, 1884. At that time, men and women made bread daily in their homes. Packaged bread, as we have today, was unknown. Baking was a time-consuming task, especially when it was done daily. On September 20, 1884, Reed received a patent for her invention.

ANNA M. MANGIN

Anna M. Mangin developed a special kind of pastry fork in 1891. She received a patent for this device on March 1, 1892. To make pastries, such as cookies and pie crusts, cooks used to mix the dough with their hands. Mangin's fork helped to mix together butter and flour for pastries without the cook having to touch the ingredients. The fork could also be used to beat eggs, mash potatoes, and prepare salad dressings.

SARA E.
GOODE

(1850–?)

✦

Sara E. Goode, born into slavery in 1850, was the first African American woman inventor noted by the United States Patent and Trademark Office. She was a teenager during the Civil War years (1861–1865). After the Emancipation Proclamation of January 1, 1863, her life slowly improved. She attended one of the schools that were opened for newly liberated African Americans.

Yet, like all African Americans, Sara found that the fruits of her training remained a dream. She was denied the right to vote. Most of her friends and family lived in poverty. Segregated in every aspect of life, she heard almost daily about violent assaults on blacks by whites throughout the South. Yet, despite these harrowing conditions, Sara E. Goode believed in herself. She was determined to overcome every obstacle that stood between her and real freedom.

Goode moved out of the South and became an entrepreneur. She was the owner of a furniture store in Chicago. She bought the furniture from a local manufacturer. But as time went on, she had a problem. Her customers became dissatisfied because much of the furniture

14

was poorly made. Then it dawned on Sara that she could make better-quality furniture herself. Soon she was imagining how new kinds of furniture could fill her customers' needs.

She noticed that her customers had little living space in their homes and apartments. Goode had the idea of inventing a bed that overnight guests could sleep on at night and fold up during the day. Then it could be used as a table. Her design looked much like an antique rolltop desk. She called it a cabinet-bed. It was the perfect solution for anyone who had limited living space. It was functional and inexpensive.

After laying out drawings of her invention, she created a model of it. Then she applied for a patent for her cabinet-bed. Goode described her invention in her patent application, filed on November 13, 1883:

> The objects of this invention are, first, to provide a folding bed of novel construction; second, to provide for counterbalancing the weight of the folding sections of the bed, so that they may be easily raised or lowered in folding or unfolding the bed; third, to provide for holding the hinged or folding sections securely in place when the bed is unfolded, and fourth, to provide an automatic auxiliary support for the bedding at the middle when the bed is unfolded.[1]

She received the patent on July 14, 1885, becoming the first African American woman inventor recorded by the United States Patent and Trademark Office.

In truth, many other African American women had created inventions before Goode, but the patents were assigned to slave holders. Prior to the ratification of the Fourteenth Amendment, which gave citizenship to African Americans, they were considered to be property. As a consequence, their inventions were considered to be property of the slave holder, too.

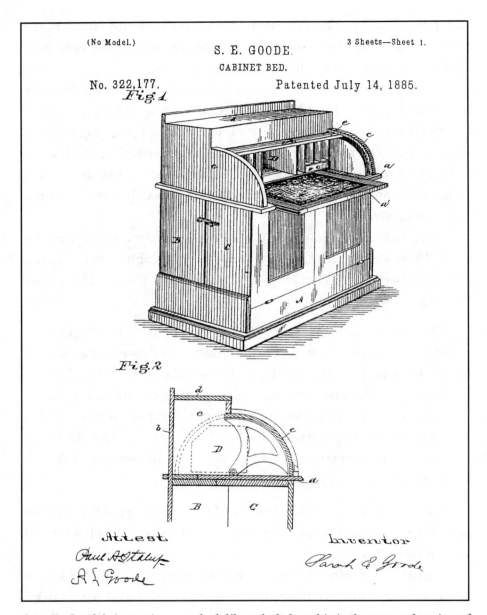

Sara E. Goode's invention may look like a desk, but this is the patent drawing of her cabinet-bed.

Little else is known about the life of Sara E. Goode. We do not know when or where she died. But her pioneering efforts are important because they forecasted that other African American women would develop and patent unique inventions.

SEEING THE PROBLEM

JULIA T. HAMMONDS

Julia T. Hammonds knew how much time and effort knitting took and she wanted to work faster, so she invented a tool to keep yarn in place. She applied for a patent for her invention, apparatus for holding yarn skeins, on September 4, 1896. In those days, knitting was not a hobby as it is today. Women knitted to keep their children in clothes and their husbands warm, but the task would take longer when the yarn got tangled. They would have to stop their work and sometimes begin again, but not with Hammonds's invention. Her ingenuity saved women time and effort.

BENJAMIN

(? – ?)

◆

By 1877, some twenty years after the Civil War, prejudice against blacks had reached a new high. White oppression eroded the power of black voters. Lynching became common. But no one could take away the dramatic gains that blacks had made as students and teachers.

Even before the Civil War, courageous individuals defied the laws against teaching blacks to read. There were private elementary schools for blacks in the North. The few black high schools and colleges included the Institute for Colored Youth in Philadelphia (later, Cheyney State Teacher's College), founded in 1837; Lincoln University in Lincoln, Pennsylvania, founded in 1854; and Wilberforce University in Wilberforce, Ohio, founded in 1856.

After the war, several more black colleges were founded. Howard University and Howard University Medical School in Washington, D.C., were notable. They quickly became symbols of black pride and hope for the future.

Miriam E. Benjamin was a schoolteacher in Washington, D.C. As a schoolteacher, Benjamin got up early to stoke the wood-burning

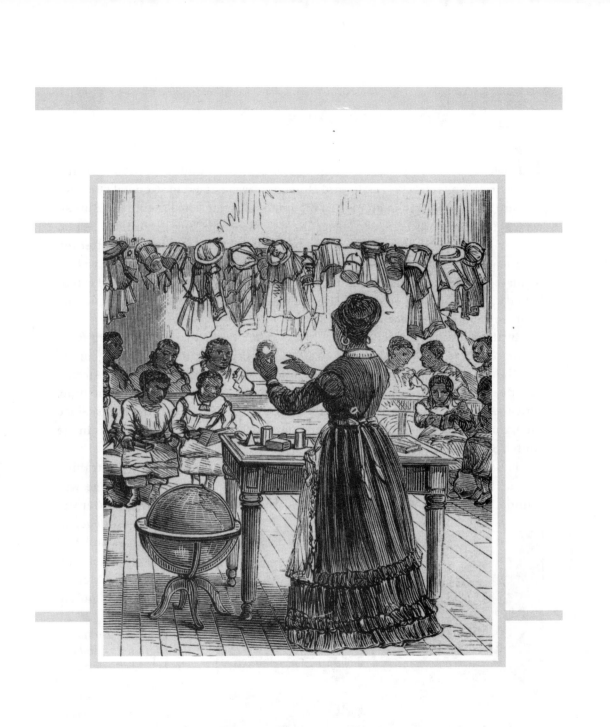

SCHOOLS OF OUR OWN

Howard University in Washington, D.C., was founded in 1867 during Reconstruction (1867–1877). Howard University was named for General Oliver O. Howard, a founder and head of the Freedmen's Bureau. The Freedmen's Bureau was established by the U.S. War Department by an act of Congress in 1865. Its aim was to provide assistance to the newly emancipated blacks of the South after the American Civil War. The bureau furnished food and medical supplies, as well as regulated wages and working conditions, supervised land distribution, and established schools for former slaves. The College of Medicine at Howard opened its doors in 1868, three years after the Civil War ended.

By this time, newly freed black people were migrating to the nation's capital in record numbers. The founders of Howard University recognized their burgeoning health care needs. The mission of the College of Medicine was to train African American students to be competent and compassionate physicians. At the time, African Americans were barred from attending most white medical schools. Since then, Howard has trained a large percentage of African American physicians in the United States and other countries.

Following the lead of Howard University and the growing need for trained African American doctors across the country, Meharry Medical College was founded in 1876 at Nashville, Tennessee, as the medical division of Central Tennessee College, an institution established by the Freedmen's Aid Society of the Methodist Episcopal Church.

Freedmen's Hospital, the original hospital of Howard University. It was the training ground for many of the country's African American doctors.

stove in the school, and instructed several grades in one room. At night, she wrote her lesson plans and graded papers. Her lively mind was always at work. One day, perhaps as she was doing her chores, she had a bright idea for a gong and signal chair. What if students could signal her from their chairs?

In her patent application, Benjamin described how this idea could be used for other workers. It was a way "to reduce the expenses of hotels, by decreasing the number of waiters and attendants, to add to the convenience and comfort of guests, and to obviate the necessity of hand-clapping or calling aloud to obtain service."[1] Customers would simply touch a button, which instantly gave a signal on the back or front of the chair to call the waiter. Consequently, a waiter would be able to serve more guests.

Benjamin conducted a patent search to determine if someone had already been assigned a patent for this idea. She needed a patent lawyer to review the search and an engineer to determine how the product could be built. She was awarded the patent on July 17, 1888.

The chair was advertised. Then Benjamin found that she had a surprising customer for it: the United States House of Representatives. Formerly, the representatives clapped their hands to signal their "pages," the boys who ran their errands and delivered their messages. With Benjamin's invention, representatives simply pressed a button on their chair, ringing a small gong and displaying a signal on the back of the chair. Now, the pages could be summoned without disturbing the House proceedings.

In 1890, Benjamin left her schoolroom and started working as a clerk in the United States Census Office. She returned to teaching again in 1892, 1894, and 1895. She was one of the four women on Henry Baker's list of colored inventors in the United States. There is no information on what happened to Benjamin after 1895.

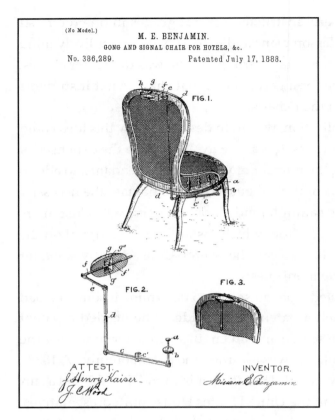

On the back of Miriam E. Benjamin's chair is a small bell to use for signaling waiters or the pages in the United States Congress.

SMALL IMPROVEMENTS COUNT

LYDIA D. NEWMAN

Some inventors such as Miriam Benjamin develop entirely unique objects; others improve on older inventions. Lydia D. Newman of New York City, for example, improved on the design of a brush and received a patent on November 15, 1898. In her patent application of July 11, 1898, Newman wrote: "The object of the invention is to provide a new and improved hair-brush which is simple and durable in construction, very effective when in use, and arranged to permit conveniently cleaning the brush whenever desired."[2] Present-day brushes are quite similar to Newman's design.

PART TWO

INTO THE NEW CENTURY

Madame C.J.
WALKER

(1867–1919)

✦

Madame C. J. Walker grew up in poverty, unable to read or write, surviving one hardship after another.

She was born in Louisiana in 1867, one year before Congress passed the Fourteenth Amendment granting blacks full citizenship. Her parents, Minerva and Owen Breedlove, were former slaves. They named her Sarah. From sunrise to sunset, she worked in the cotton fields near the shores of the Mississippi River. Her parents died before she was six, leaving her older sister, Louvinia, to care for her.

Married at the age of fourteen to Moses McWilliams, Sarah was a widow by the time she was twenty. Some sources report that Moses McWilliams was killed in a race riot in 1888; however, there is no proof to support this claim. Others report that he was lynched. Again, this cannot be documented. There were a number of lynchings in the South during this time. Scarcely more than a teenager, all that Sarah had was their child, Lelia, who she called her "wealth." From 1887 to 1905, moving with Lelia to Vicksburg, Mississippi, then to St. Louis,

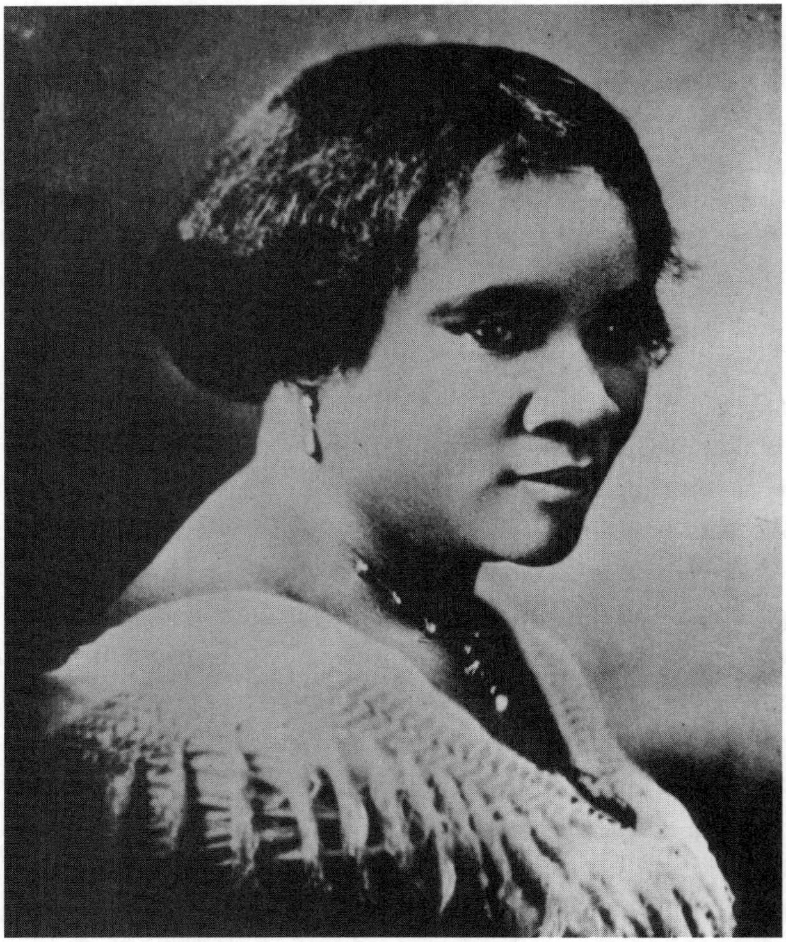

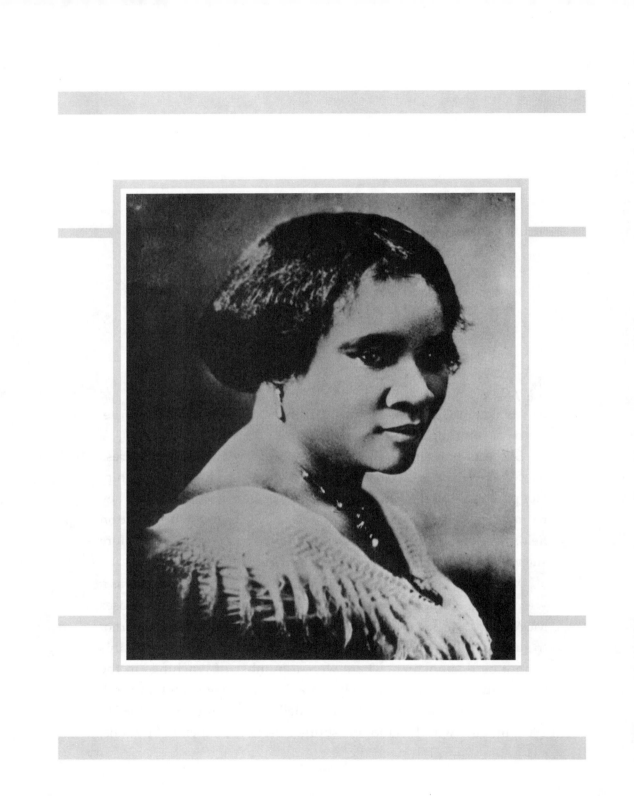

Sarah supported herself and her daughter by working as a washer-woman for white families.

Still a young woman, Sarah had already faced enough catastrophes for a lifetime. Then her hair began to fall out. She began experimenting with various mineral and animal oils to find a remedy.

"One night I had a dream," she would say later. "A man appeared to me and told me what to mix up for my hair. Some of the remedy was grown in Africa, but I sent for it, put it on my scalp, and in a few weeks my hair was coming in faster than it had ever fallen out." An advertisement for her product read, "For long and beautiful hair use Madame C. J. Walker's wonderful Hair Grower, as it is one of the most wonderful discoveries of the age and is positively guaranteed to grow hair or money refunded." She claimed that her product "cures the scalp of all diseases and stops the hair from falling out, and starts it at once to grow."[1]

In 1905, feeling revived, Sarah moved to Denver to help her sister. She started selling her secret hair-care formula to her new neighbors, and she married C. J. Walker. She liked being called Madame C. J. Walker, and she used that name for the rest of her life.

In 1908, leaving Mr. Walker behind, Madame Walker and Lelia moved to Pittsburgh, Pennsylvania. In 1910, Madame C. J. Walker moved her offices from Denver and Pittsburgh to Indianapolis, Indiana. A plant was constructed and became the headquarters for the Walker enterprise. It was called the Walker College of Hair Culture and Walker Manufacturing Company. The company provided employment for some three thousand people. Madame Walker called her employees "hair culturists," "scalp specialists," and "beauty culturists."

Business thrived. The Walker system even found its way to Europe. Josephine Baker, the singing and dancing sensation of Paris, had her hair styled using the Walker method. Her hair became a walking advertisement for Madame Walker and started a fad called the "Baker-Fix."

Madame Walker had founded a beauty school in Pittsburgh to teach the Walker system. She called it the Lelia College of Beauty. She opened her second beauty school in 1910 in Indianapolis. While Lelia helped sell the products through the mail, Walker toured the country, encouraging other women to buy Walker products and to be as independent as she was.

"I am a woman who came from the cotton fields of the South promoted from there to the washtub. Then I was promoted to the kitchen, and from there I promoted myself into the business of manufacturing hair goods and preparations."[2] This was Madame C. J. Walker's introduction when she presented herself to the National Negro Business League's 1912 convention.

She surrounded herself with loyal, capable workers and became one of the nation's largest employers of African American women. Her employees often went to their clients' homes to style their hair. The

Madame C. J. Walker, the first African American woman millionaire.

Becoming A Leader

Madame Walker hired thousands of agents, primarily other African American women, to sell and demonstrate the Walker system door-to-door across the country. By 1925, more than 25,000 agents worked for her. Walker required her agents to sign contracts that specified that they would use her company's products and methods and follow the rules for health and cleanliness mandated by state cosmetology laws. *The Crisis*, the magazine of the National Association for the Advancement of Colored People (NAACP), believed that Madame C. J. Walker had influenced the "personal habits and appearance of millions of human beings."

> ✦ **Cosmetology** is the study of the skin, hair and nails, or the art of using makeup.

employees dressed uniformly in spotless, starched white shirts and long black skirts. Walker encouraged them to be inventors, too. Several women emulated Walker and were highly successful in their hair-care business.

Madame Walker at last began to enjoy her success as a millionaire. Vertner Tandy, an African American architect, built a mansion for her, called Villa Lewaro, at Irvington-on-the-Hudson, New York. The building cost $250,000, which was quite a sum in 1917. The twenty-room mansion cost $500,000 to furnish.

Walker gave generously to the NAACP, Tuskegee Institute, and various charities that supported black orphans. She also gave generous gifts to the Daytona Normal and Institute for Negro Girls, founded by her friend, Mary McLeod Bethune. Madame Walker provided scholarships for students at Palmer Memorial Institute, a private high school for blacks in Sedalia, North Carolina, founded by her friend, Charlotte Hawkins Brown.

Refusing to heed the advice of her doctors that her hypertension required an extended rest from her active schedule, Madame C. J. Walker became seriously ill in St. Louis. She returned to New York. When Madame Walker died suddenly on May 25, 1919, her empire was at its height. In her will, she left the business to her daughter, as well as $100,000 to build a school for girls in West Africa. She also made sure that the Madame C. J. Walker Manufacturing Company would always have a woman president.

Madame Walker's daughter died suddenly in 1931, leaving the remaining estate to the NAACP. Today, the headquarters of the Walker Manufacturing Company is in Tuskegee, Alabama.

A N N I E T U R N B O
MALONE
(1 8 6 9 – 1 9 5 7)

✦

Annie Minerva Turnbo Malone invented hair and skin products a few years before Madame C. J. Walker. Like Madame Walker, Annie became a millionaire by successfully marketing her products.

Born to Robert and Isabella Cook Turnbo on August 9, 1869, in the small town of Metropolis, Illinois, Annie was the tenth of eleven children. While the other children were playing games, Annie entertained herself by braiding strings attached to a Coca-Cola bottle. She had fun pretending that she was braiding real hair.

Annie attended Peoria, Illinois High School, where she discovered that she had an interest in physical science. Her favorite subject was chemistry. But she never outgrew her fascination with hair care. She often braided other girls' hair after school.

> ✦ **Chemistry** is the science of substances. Chemists discover what's in the substances and how to combine those elements in different ways.

Annie's friends used goose fat, soap, and heavy oils to straighten their hair. Annie noticed that these mixtures were often damaging, causing the

31

girls to lose their hair and develop scalp problems. Annie believed there must be a way to straighten hair without hurting it. If there was, she could figure it out.

She spent countless hours experimenting with ingredients that did not harm the hair and scalp. Soon she was spending so much time on her project that she dropped out of school. Her mission became clear: She was going to give African American women their own beauty products. And she did. Annie started her business with only $5, but within ten years she developed and manufactured a series of hair products, deodorants, skin creams, pressing oils, and other toiletries. These products were sold in all of the major U.S. cities, Europe, South America, and many African countries. Turnbo became the major stakeholder in the black cosmetics and beauty industry.

In 1900, Turnbo patented the first pressing comb to iron hair. In 1902, she moved to St. Louis, Missouri, seeking new opportunities. She set up shop and hired employees as agents. Turnbo and her agents went door to door, selling her products and giving free beauty treatments to demonstrate their quality.

What did she name her product line? She chose a West African word, *Poro,* meaning physical and spiritual growth. Black newspapers advertised her hair-straightening and conditioning products. But she always said the best advertisement was a satisfied customer. Her agents were required to provide a twenty-four-hour turnaround time in shipping products to customers.

Along the way, Annie got married, but was soon divorced. As a single woman, she continued with her plan to build up her business. Its phenomenal growth was attributed to her shrewdness, persistence, hard work, and commitment. In 1917, she purchased an entire city block and built a multi-million-dollar complex. She chose to include a vocational school, which she named Poro College.

Poro College trained African American beauticians, barbers, and salespeople. This school became the first institution to teach

BLAZING A TRAIL

Poro College also became a cultural institution for African Americans in St. Louis. There was a theater, an auditorium, and a cafeteria. Entertainers including Roland Hayes and Bessie Smith offered concerts at Poro's plush concert hall. In a short time, Poro College was franchised in more than fifty cities. More than fifty thousand African American cosmetologists were trained at Poro, including Madame C. J. Walker, who later made a fortune of her own, but died in 1919 at the height of her fame (see page 25.)

cosmetology for the black consumer. The college had classrooms for teaching beauty culture, barbershops for cutting African American men's hair, and well-equipped laboratories for developing new hair and skin products.

By 1920, Annie Turnbo Malone was worth more than $14 million. Six years later, she had more than 75,000 agents who sold her products door to door throughout the United States, the Caribbean, and other countries. In the late 1920s, though, Poro was faced with a series of problems, including the historic stock market crash of 1929 followed by the Great Depression. By the end of the day on October 24, 1929, the stock market had lost $4 billion dollars—money that was people's life savings. It took years for the country to recover.

By 1932, Malone courageously decided to put the personal and business challenges she faced in St. Louis behind her and move to Chicago. She purchased a manufacturing plant in Chicago's white manufacturing district and set up shop on a street that became known as Poro Block. Annie Turnbo Malone died in Chicago's Provident Hospital on May 10, 1957, of a stroke. She was eighty-seven years old.

ROGER ARLINER
YOUNG, PH.D.

(1889–1964)

✦

Roger Arliner Young was born in Clifton Forge, Virginia, and grew up in Burgettstown, Pennsylvania. She was a quiet child who often played by herself, making up games and carefully collecting sticks and stones. She liked nothing better than being outdoors, looking at the trees, sky, and wildlife in the countryside. She was more curious about nature than she was about other things in school.

Young spent several years working various jobs before she could afford to go to college, but she was determined to go to school and learn more about the world she loved. She eventually entered Howard University. In 1921, she took her first science course from Ernest Everett Just, a prominent African American biologist and head of the zoology department at Howard. Although Young did not have the best grades, Dr. Just

✦ **Zoology** is the study of animal life.

✦ A **biologist** studies plants and animals.

saw promise in her and served as her mentor. She received a bachelor of science degree from Howard in 1923. Immediately after

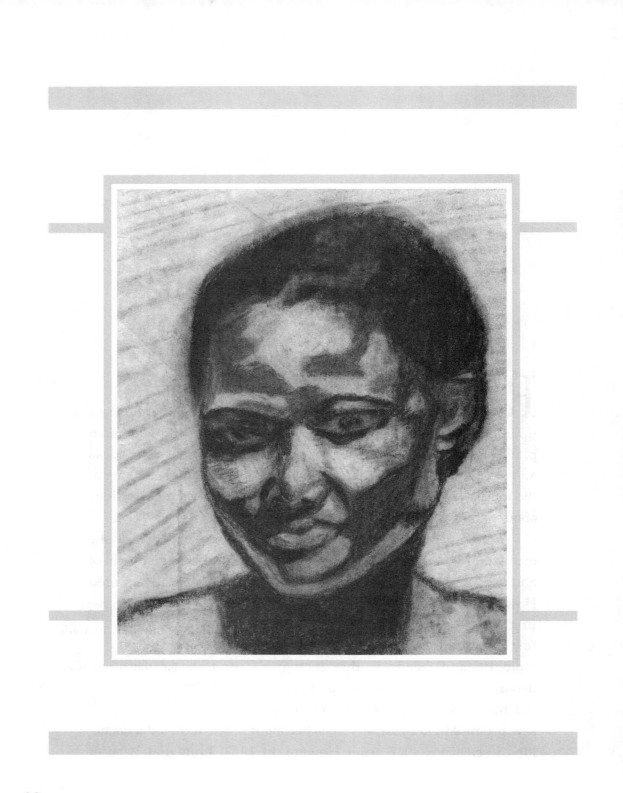

graduation, she was hired as an assistant professor of zoology at Howard.

Dr. Just encouraged Young to pursue advanced degrees, even helping her find financial assistance to attend graduate school. Following his advice, she went to Chicago and enrolled as a part-time student at the University of Chicago.

At the University of Chicago, Young's professors recognized her talent and dedication to scientific research. Young began her scientific career at the Marine Biological Laboratory in Woods Hole, Massachusetts, the leading biological research institution in the United States. She became the first African American woman to conduct and publish research in her field. Young was elected to Sigma Xi, an honor society. She published her first article "On the Excretory Apparatus in Paramecium," in *Science,* a well-respected journal, in September 1924.

In 1924, Young returned to Howard to do research with her mentor, Ernest Everett Just. He directed her research in the study of structures that control salt concentration in paramecium. Young wrote numerous scientific articles on the effects of direct and indirect radiation on sea urchin eggs. In 1926, she was awarded a master of science in zoology, becoming one of the few African American women to hold an advanced degree.

Young returned to teaching in Howard's zoology department. Early in 1929, she stood in for Dr. Just as head of the department while he worked on a project in Europe. Young returned to Chicago to start work on her doctorate. Facing numerous problems, she failed her qualifying exams in 1930. She was devastated. At the time, she had no money to care for her invalid mother. She left Chicago and did not tell anyone of her whereabouts.

She finally returned to Howard as a teacher and continued working at Woods Hole in the summer. In 1935, she was fired from her position after missing several classes. Young took her firing as an opportunity. She remembered that one cannot give up when faced

THE MENTOR

Roger Arliner Young may not have accomplished all that she did without the help and encouragement of a Howard University professor, Dr. Ernest Everett Just. Although Young struggled to get good grades, Dr. Just saw promise in her. He felt that with the right guidance her potential as a student would soon be fulfilled.

Dr. Just was not only a well-respected Howard University professor; he was also a leading scientist in zoology. His research led to the idea that life existed only when all cell parts worked together as a unit. This idea challenged the thinking of some eminent biologists. His example of excellence helped Dr. Young reach her own potential.

Roger Arliner Young's mentor, Ernest Everett Just.

with adversity. From 1935 to 1938, Young published four scientific papers. She returned to school to work on her doctorate at the University of Pennsylvania. In 1940, Young became the first African American woman to receive a Ph.D. in zoology.

After receiving her doctorate, Dr. Young, like many other African Americans, sought employment at leading research institutions, but was rejected. Undaunted, she decided to share her talents with African American students and encourage them to pursue careers in science and technology. Consequently, Dr. Young taught at the North Carolina College for Negroes and at Shaw University, North Carolina, from 1940 to 1947.

✦ **Technology** is the science of practical things.

Dr. Young continued teaching at primarily black colleges in Texas, Louisiana, and Mississippi during the 1950s. While in Mississippi, her mental health failed and she was hospitalized at the state mental asylum. Discharged from the asylum in 1962, she went to Southern University in New Orleans. Dr. Young died poor and alone on November 9, 1964.

MARJORIE STEWART
JOYNER, PH.D.
(1896–1994)

✦

Marjorie Stewart Joyner, the granddaughter of former slaves, was born in Virginia's Blue Ridge Mountains in the town of Monterey on October 24, 1896. At age six, Marjorie's parents divorced, and she moved to Chicago with her mother, who made sure Marjorie got a good education. She graduated from Chicago Christian High School and later married Dr. Robert Joyner, a podiatrist. Eventually, her mother-in-law encouraged her to study at one of Madame C. J. Walker's schools.

But there was one problem. Joyner explained:

> I was working for Mrs. Walker, and, you know . . . we operators might put in a very nice hairdo, but it would never last very long, and in the morning, a customer who looked beautiful when she left my care [later] looked like an accident going some place to happen. It is important for a woman to show that she takes care of her hair, and that was in my mind when I invented the machine. It would allow a woman to look neat [for days], and that is important!

41

She called her invention the permanent-wave machine.

"It all came to me in the kitchen when I was making a pot roast one day, looking at these long, thin rods that held the pot roast together and heated it up from the inside."[1] Pot roast rods were often used by cooks to speed up the cooking of a beef roast. Thin rods were inserted into the pot roast to hold it together and for cooking evenly. Marjorie Stewart Joyner said, "I figured you could use them like hair rollers, then heat them up to cook a permanent curl into the hair."[2]

Joyner began to experiment. She hooked sixteen pencil-shaped pot roast rods to an old-fashioned hair dryer hood and joined them together to draw electricity through a single electrical cord. Joyner was successful in developing her invention and used it at her shop, Marjorie's Beauty Salon, located in the basement of her home at 5607 S. Wabash Avenue.

Joyner improved the permanent-wave machine when customers complained that it was uncomfortable. She wrote: "An object of the invention is the construction of a simple and efficient scalp protector used upon the patron's head during the process of waving her hair."[3]

Joyner almost missed the deadline for patenting her invention. She didn't realize that she even needed a patent until 1928, which was nearly three years after she invented the perming machine. If she had waited a few months, she would have been ineligible to patent the device. On November 17, 1928, Joyner received patents for the machines she designed to improve the Walker System of Hair Care. Because Marjorie was an employee of Madame Walker's at the time, the patents were assigned to the Walker Company.

The permanent-wave machine looked like a bird cage on a stand with several instruments hanging from the dome. It was an instant sensation and appealed to countless hair stylists across the country. It could wave the hair of both white and black people in the popular style called the Marcel Wave.

Joyner spent the difficult years during the Great Depression teaching grooming, "no matter how hard times were." She recalled: "I worked with both men and women. I told them to keep up good grooming, that a good personal appearance helps people get and hold jobs. I even taught them how to walk and sit down. People need to make their own opportunities, and appearance is important."[4] Madame C. J. Walker, owner of the Walker Manufacturing Company, appreciated and respected Joyner's ingenuity and dedication. Joyner became the national supervisor of the nationwide chain of beauty schools operated by the Madame C. J. Walker Manufacturing Company.

Later in life, Joyner returned to school and earned a Ph.D. in humanities. While she received many awards during her lifetime, she was especially proud of the award she received on November 3, 1989, by the Patent Law Association of Chicago. Chicagoans regarded her with the respect of a first lady. "If I can take pot roast rods and have a one-of-a-kind invention, believe me, people can do what they set their minds to do."[5] She died in 1994, two years before her one hundredth birthday.

THE ENTREPRENEURS

Madame C. J. Walker, Marjorie Stewart Joyner, and Annie Turnbo Malone showed women how to become empowered through business. With little expense, they were able to start prosperous businesses. Beauty shops could be found in the largest cities and smallest towns of America.

Going to the beauty shop became one of the few luxuries that African American women had at the time and a wonderful way to relax and be pampered. In this single-sex environment, women could discuss health problems, family relationships, parenthood, men and community issues. It was a source of powerful sisterly support, as well as a source of beauty, training, and employment.

PART THREE

MODERN TIMES

MARY BEATRICE DAVIDSON
KENNER
(B. 1912)

MILDRED AUSTIN
SMITH
(1916–1993)

◆

Inventing seems to run in the Davidson family. At a young age, sisters Mary Beatrice Davidson Kenner and Mildred Austin Smith were encouraged by their father to find a better way to do things. Mr. Davidson inspired his children through his words and example to believe that they could do anything if they put their minds to it. As an inventor himself, Mr. Davidson encouraged his daughters to pursue science and to not limit themselves. He also told the children about their family history and the contributions of family members.

Mary grew up to be one of the most prolific African American women inventors. Even at age six, Mary showed a special ability for invention. The screeching of the bedroom door each time someone came in or out of her room disturbed her, so she put a small amount of oil on the door hinge. The hinge stopped making noise. By age seven, Mary was intensely curious and showed a particular love for gadgets, disassembling them to see how they worked.

Kenner began inventing in the early 1950s. She was sensitive to the needs of the elderly, sick, and physically challenged, and wanted them to be more self-reliant. Invalid walkers give extra support to people who have difficulty walking. Kenner invented a pocket for the walkers that could hold important things such as medical equipment or a purse. She spent a number of years laying out her design, finding materials, and developing her invention. On May 18, 1976, Kenner received a patent for a carrier attachment for invalid walkers.

Always thinking up new ideas, Kenner also developed a bathroom tissue holder. While living in Williamsburg, Virginia, she received a patent for her invention, on October 19, 1982. Kenner described her invention as "a holder for retaining the free or loose end of a roll of bathroom tissue or toilet paper in accessible position spaced away from the periphery of the bathroom tissue or toilet paper roll."[1]

Kenner continued inventing. She patented her back washer mounted on a shower wall and bathtub on September 29, 1987. This invention is attached to the shower wall and washes hard-to-reach places such as the back.

Her sister was intrigued by invention as well. On October 28, 1980, Mildred Austin Smith developed a game to explore family relationships. Smith received a patent for her family relationships card game.

Smith recalled the background of her game: "In earlier generations, the social organization of the family was such as to result in the exposure of young children to older relatives outside their immediate family as a natural consequence of repeated personal contact and interaction."[2] This was just what Smith was hoping to inspire. Players learned family members' names and how they are related to them.

THE TOYMAKERS

For centuries, African American women and men have created toys for their children. This tradition dates back to Africa, where the most prized gift a child could receive for any special occasion was a toy crafted by a parent or relative.

- ✦ **Lydia M. Holmes** invented the knockdown wheeled toy.
- ✦ **Margaret Cheetham** created a fun toy that made a cat chase a rat.
- ✦ **Shereen Emde** made dolls for Kwanzaa, an African American holiday.
- ✦ **Ruby Jackson** developed African American dominoes and a puzzle featuring prominent African American figures.

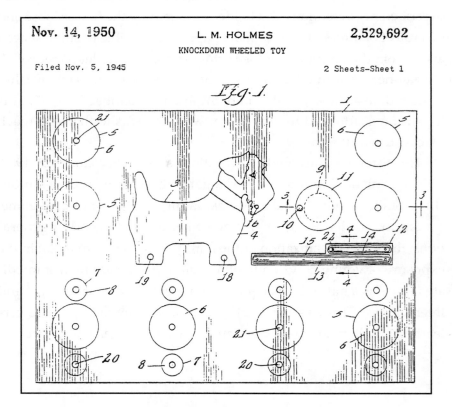

One of many toys invented by an African American woman.

BESSIE BLOUNT
GRIFFIN

(1913–?)

✦

Bessie Blount Griffin did not set out to become an inventor. However, she became a trailblazer whose invention improved the lives of injured World War II veterans. Griffin was born in Hickory, Virginia, in 1913. As a child, she showed an interest in helping the elderly and invalid. There is little known about her family or her childhood. She left the South to attend Union Junior College in Cranford, New Jersey, and Panzer College of Physical Education in East Orange, New Jersey. Along the way, she studied physical therapy in Chicago.

Working as a physical therapist and teacher of physical therapy at the Bronx Hospital in New York City, Griffin encountered many men whose legs and arms were amputated because of injuries suffered in World War II (1941–1945). Thousands of American soldiers were injured and/or disabled during the war. She believed that amputees could lead useful

✦ A **physical therapist** uses exercise and massage to heal people's injuries.

51

lives and should not be cast aside to be dependent and helpless. Consequently, Griffin dedicated herself to rehabilitating patients. Her dedication and success caused patients and co-workers to refer to her as "Wonder Woman."

In 1948, Griffin began developing her automatic invalid feeder after a doctor sarcastically told her, "If you really want to help these men, develop something so they can feed themselves." Not one to back down from a challenge, this comment motivated Griffin. That night, Griffin stayed up, jotting down ideas for her invention. Some evenings she stayed up all night working in her kitchen as she developed this device. She prayed she would be successful. She sought advice from the Veterans Administration Office, but received no direction and support. One official told her, "You are just wasting your time on these crippled and disabled folks."

Bessie was undaunted by the lack of assistance and negative comments. They fueled her desire to be successful. While some people would have easily given up and abandoned their plans, Griffin remembered that "Nothing beats a failure but a try."

Griffin contacted her congressional representative, who set up an appointment with Paul B. Maguson, chief medical director of Bronx Hospital. He called her invention impractical. "Stick to nursing and make these men comfortable," he advised. She sought assistance from the doctor who first planted the idea for the invention, but he discouraged her, saying, "I was only joking with you." She, like most inventors, did not pay attention to discouraging remarks, choosing to pursue her dream and make it a reality.

Griffin finally applied for a patent for the automatic invalid feeder on March 29, 1948. After three years and $3,000 of her personal savings, she received the patent on April 24, 1951.

This invention had the potential to revolutionize many people's lives. Griffin describes it in her patent application: "A primary object of the invention is to provide an apparatus for enabling invalids,

HELPING OTHERS

IOLA O. CARTER

Another caring inventor like Bessie Blount Griffin was Iola O. Carter. Carter invented a nursery chair that could be folded up and used in a car. Like Griffin, Carter wanted to make people's lives better. Parents could use the chair in their house and have a safe place for their child in the car, since the chair could be carried like a traveling case.

JOAN CLARK

Joan Clark also found a simple but effective way to help people. She developed a medicine tray with several compartments for patients' medicine. Nurses could place a patient's medicine in the tray and dispense it when needed.

convalescents, and all persons suffering from a temporary or permanent impairment of the use of the arms and hands to conveniently and in comfort drink fluid from cups or bowls supported by the device."[1]

Griffin tried to market the device to Bronx Hospital, but no one was interested. Unsuccessful efforts were made to promote the invention to the Veterans Administration. She couldn't find anyone interested in purchasing her invention.

Like other scientists and inventors, she did not allow this rejection to stop her. She continued developing useful aids for patients. In the meantime, she patented a simpler device called a portable receptacle support, which also allowed people to feed themselves.

In 1952, after numerous attempts to market the feeding devices, Griffin offered her invention to the French government, and it was gladly accepted. An agreement was signed at the French Embassy in 1952. In her press statement, Griffin said she felt that she had contributed to the progress of her people by "proving that a black woman can invent something for the benefit of humankind."

Griffin would often remind her patients that "There is always someone worse off than you. You may not have legs, arms, or feet, but you cannot wallow in self-pity, for you must be self-reliant."

WRIGHT, M.D.

(B . 1 9 1 9)

◆

J ane Cooke Wright was the third generation of physicians in her family. She was born in New York City to Dr. Louis Tompkins Wright and Corinne Cooke Wright, an elementary school teacher. Dr. Louis Wright, a graduate of Harvard University Medical School, was a well-respected surgeon at Harlem Hospital, the first African American on staff. It was no surprise that young Jane absorbed the qualities that lead to success. She saw how his intellect, discipline, commitment, and big ideas made a difference.

Young Jane Wright loved mathematics and science. Naturally, she enjoyed toys and play, but she also thought it was fun to solve mathematical problems and conduct scientific experiments. Early on, while she attended the Ethical Culture School and Fieldston High School in New York City, she decided that she would attend college and make a difference, too.

Her interests went further than just math and science. She was on the swim team at Fieldston and set records for the 100-yard

HER FATHER'S FOOTSTEPS

Jane found in her father an outstanding mentor. He made the world of medicine and research as familiar to her as playgrounds are to some children. Going with her father to Harlem Hospital, Jane discovered the importance of caring for other people. Watching him work as chairman of the board of the National Association for the Advancement of Colored People (NAACP) reinforced her identity as an African American. He worked for thirty years at Harlem Hospital, and was the first black doctor ever to work there. Some doctors protested, but he went on to become the director of surgery. Dr. Wright invented several surgical devices and was a respected cancer researcher.

Jane Cooke Wright found a great example of excellence in her own family: her father, Louis Wright.

breaststroke and 100-yard freestyle. She worked at everything she did with intensity. She expressed her creativity in modern dance.

After graduating from high school in 1938, Jane Wright was accepted at prestigious Smith College in Massachusetts. At first, she found it difficult to select a major. Everything from German and French to mathematics and painting was exciting to her. But by the end of her sophomore year, she realized that her favorite subject was physics and decided to pursue medicine.

As a member of the varsity swim team, Wright set records that lasted years. She passed her comprehensive examinations in seven subjects with highest distinction and graduated with highest honors in 1942.

In 1942, few females were enrolled in medical school. Wright wanted to attend Harvard University, but it did not yet accept women into medical school. She was awarded a four-year scholarship to New York Medical College. Her father, who had suffered severe damage to his lungs during an enemy gas attack in World War I (1914–1918), was increasingly disabled by tuberculosis. Although this illness caused financial hardships for the Wright family, Jane's mother encouraged her to continue her education.

+ An **intern** is an assistant doctor in training in a hospital.

+ A **resident** is a doctor in advance training in a special field of medicine.

+ A **psychiatrist** is a doctor who deals with mental, emotional, or behavior problems.

+ **Chemotherapy** is the treatment of cancer with chemical elements.

After medical school, Jane did her internship in internal medicine at Bellevue Hospital and two residencies at Harlem Hospital. Along the way, she married David Dallas Jones, a lawyer. They became the proud parents of two daughters: Jane, who became a psychiatrist, and Alison, who earned a Ph.D. in clinical psychology.

In 1948, Dr. Louis Wright established the Cancer Research Foundation to study chemotherapy treatments at Harlem Hospital with the support of grants from the National Cancer Institute and another funder. Cancer research was just beginning, and some people viewed practitioners of chemotherapy as dreamers or fakes.

Dr. Jane Wright joined her father in his pioneering research. This gave her a special chance to learn about the innovations in cancer treatment. Before the 1940s, cancer treatments included corrosive acids, arsenic paste, and ground-up toads. These treatments were unsuccessful and often caused excruciating pain for the patients.

Dr. Wright rolled up her sleeves and approached her work with her usual intensity and a new mission to find an effective cancer treatment. Fund-raising for chemotherapy research was difficult, but through the National Institutes of Health, the National Cancer Center, and the United States Public Health Center, the federal government provided much of the support for the Wrights' research.

In 1952, Dr. Louis Wright suffered a heart attack and died. Dr. Jane Wright continued her work at New York University as a professor of research surgery and the director of chemotherapy. During the 1950s and 1960s, she treated cancer patients with various types of anticancer drugs, gaining more knowledge and experience with new treatments that prolonged patients' lives. Still, she hoped to find a way to help people with cancer live even longer.

A GIANT LEAP

Dr. Wright's research led to further advances in cancer treatment, in the ways drugs were given and dosages were determined. Her research showed that giving drugs by mouth or general injection was not the most effective way to fight cancer cells. Injection into the specific major artery and vein of the cancerous area worked much better. She also concluded that patients should start out on low doses and work up to higher doses. She was among the first researchers to recognize that treatment must vary from person to person.

In 1967, Dr. Wright returned to New York Medical College as professor of surgery and associate dean, a first for an African American female. There, as director of the cancer research laboratory, she tried a new approach to testing the drugs.

In her biggest breakthrough, Dr. Jane Wright surgically removed pieces of a patient's cancerous tumor and grew these pieces, called tissues, in her laboratory. Then she treated them with a variety of drugs. Under a microscope, she determined the amount of damage the drugs had done to the cancer cells they were supposed to destroy. At the time, there were at least twenty anticancer drugs. Using Wright's method for testing them, cancer specialists could predict the effects of particular drugs and decide which ones worked best for each patient's cancer.

Dr. Jane Cooke Wright found her own path. She published 135 scientific papers and contributed to nine books. She was one of the seven founding members of the American Society of Clinical Oncology and the first woman elected president of the New York Cancer Society. Concerned for people everywhere, she traveled to Eastern Europe, China, the former Soviet Union, and Africa to present the latest knowledge in cancer research and treatment.

EVELYN BOYD
GRANVILLE, PH.D.

(B . 1 9 2 4)

✦

Evelyn Boyd was born in Washington, D.C., the second daughter of William and Julia Boyd. The Boyds made many sacrifices to enrich their daughters' education. They taught Evelyn and her sister that brain power knows no color or race.

As a child, Evelyn always loved mathematics. As early as elementary school, she knew she wanted to be a math teacher. To reach her goal, Evelyn worked hard in school. She was salutatorian of her junior high school class and one of five valedictorians at Dunbar Senior High School.

At Dunbar, Evelyn's interest in mathematics was supported by two mathematics teachers: Ulysses Basset, a graduate of Yale, and Mary Cromwell, a graduate of the University of Pennsylvania. They encouraged her to apply to Smith College and Mt. Holyoke in Massachusetts. Both schools were expensive and Evelyn knew she would have to get a scholarship. Evelyn was accepted by both colleges, but neither offered financial assistance. Her mother and her sister offered to pay half of her college expenses for the first year. Each

gave Evelyn $500 and other relatives chipped in $100. Additional assistance came in the form of a scholarship from African American teachers who were members of Phi Delta Kappa, a national educational society. With financial aid in place, Evelyn entered Smith College in 1941.

The other students at Smith College, a prestigious school for women, were white and came from the finest public and private schools. Evelyn knew that she could succeed at Smith because Dunbar High School had prepared her to be the best. She was at the top of her class and received financial assistance to continue her studies. She graduated in 1945 and was inducted into Phi Beta Kappa, the highest recognition of academic achievement.

After graduating from Smith, Evelyn was accepted at Yale University for graduate study. Although Smith offered her a scholarship for graduate school, she chose Yale instead. Evelyn continued to do well at Yale.

Dr. Einar Hille, a distinguished and well-known mathematician, became Evelyn's mentor and research advisor. In 1949, Yale awarded Evelyn a Ph.D. in mathematics, making her one of two African American women in the United States to receive a doctorate in mathematics.

Dr. Boyd worked as a research assistant at the New York University Institute for Mathematics and as a part-time instructor in the mathematics department at the university. She also worked as a professor at Fisk University in Nashville, Tennessee, and at North Carolina College (now North Carolina Central University). One of her students, Vivienne Malone Mayes, who received her doctorate in 1966 from the University of Texas at Austin, would say of her teacher, "I believe it was her presence and influence that account for my pursuit of advanced degrees in mathematics."

Dr. Boyd returned to Washington, D.C., in 1952, to accept a position as a mathematician at the National Bureau of Standards (NBS).

GOOD ADVICE FOR FUTURE SCIENTISTS

Get a solid foundation in algebra in order to succeed in higher math subjects related to one's major.[1]

—*Dr. Evelyn Boyd Granville*

She worked with engineers and scientists to develop missile fuses. While working at the NBS, Dr. Boyd met several mathematicians who were employed as computer programmers. During the early 1950s, the development of the computer was just beginning. Dr. Boyd was fascinated with the application of computers to scientific studies. She was offered a position with the computer company International Business Machines Corporation (IBM).

At IBM, Dr. Boyd learned computer programming. She found it challenging—an exercise in logical thinking and problem solving. Dr. Boyd's supervisor instantly recognized her brilliance, and within a year she moved to New York City to work as an IBM consultant.

✦ A **computer program** is the set of coded instructions for storing, finding, or using electronic information.

The National Aeronautics and Space Administration (NASA) awarded IBM a contract to plan, write, and maintain computer programs for the U.S. space program. As a result, IBM opened the Vanguard Computing Center in Washington, D.C. Dr. Boyd was offered the opportunity to work at the center, so she returned to Washington. In an interview, she said, "My most interesting work in mathematics came when I was part of a team of IBM mathematicians and scientists working with NASA to produce computer programs for NASA's Vanguard and Mercury space programs in the 1950s."[2]

Dr. Boyd married in 1960 and moved to Los Angeles, California. She easily found employment with the North American Aviation Company (NAA). In August 1962, she became a research specialist with the Space and Information Systems Division of NAA.

In 1967, Dr. Boyd divorced. She was appointed an assistant professor of mathematics at California State University, Los Angeles (CSULA), teaching classes in computer programming and numerical analysis.

In 1970, Dr. Boyd married Edward V. Granville, a successful real estate broker in Los Angeles. Dr. Boyd Granville retired from CSULA in March 1984 and moved to a large farm that she and her husband had purchased near Tyler, Texas. But Dr. Boyd Granville didn't retire for long. She began teaching a computer literacy class to eighth graders at the nearby Van Independent School District.

In January 1985, Dr. Boyd Granville began teaching at Texas College, a small, predominantly black, four-year college in Tyler, Texas. Currently, she is involved in a program sponsored by Dow Chemical Company. For the past two years, she has visited schools—mainly middle schools—to talk to students about the need for competent, well-trained scientists, engineers, technicians, and business planners in private industry and government. She has visited schools throughout Texas to encourage students in mathematics.

The National Academy of Sciences honored Dr. Boyd Granville in her hometown in February 1999. Dow Chemical recognized her as a "pioneer in science" and sponsored her visit to Dunbar High School for Black History Month to show students what can be achieved through the study of mathematics.

A SCIENTIST'S ADVICE TO TEACHERS

To make science meaningful, teachers should employ hands-on activities that involve making conjectures and devising ways of testing one's assumptions. To make math more interesting, students have to be shown how math is related to other academic areas and to our daily activities. Math should be presented as a problem-solving activity.[3]

—Dr. Evelyn Boyd Granville

JEWEL PLUMMER
COBB, Ph.D.
(B. 1924)

✦

Biologist Jewel Plummer Cobb was born in Chicago, Illinois, on January 17, 1924. Growing up in an upper middle-class family, she had many cultural and educational opportunities. For example, her mother took her to the ballet and to see the opera *Porgy and Bess* in New York City.

But Jewel did not take her advantages for granted. She read about African Americans in history books by historian Carter G. Woodson, writer Arna Bontemps, and anthropologist Allison Davis. From these books she learned to appreciate the black struggle for equality.

Jewel was fascinated with science and spent many days exploring the grounds of her home looking for butterflies and other insects. At an early age, she knew the scientific classification of some insects.

About her career choice Dr. Cobb says, "When I was a sophomore in high school, I had a microscope given to me in a laboratory to look through, and that was it! I said, 'That's for me, biology.'"[1] Her tenth-grade teacher at Englewood High School, one of the finest high schools in Chicago, motivated her to take classes in botany, chemistry,

and zoology. Jewel read Paul Dekruif's book, *Microbe Hunters,* and became even more interested in biology. By the time she graduated from high school, Jewel decided to become a biology teacher.

After graduating at the top of her class at Englewood, Jewel was accepted to the University of Michigan. At the time, there were few African American students there or at any historically white college or university. Despite three semesters of receiving excellent grades, Jewel realized that Michigan was not for her, in part because of the discrimination there. At the time, Michigan did not even allow African American students to live in the dormitory. Jewel made up her mind to leave Michigan and seek admission to a college that would welcome her. Hilda Davis, the dean of women at Talladega College, an historically African American institution in Alabama, recruited Jewel.

Upon arriving at Talladega, Jewel loved the caring manner of professors and students. Talladega was a small school and Jewel felt as if she were finally at home. She thrived there and was always on the honor roll.

Jewel graduated from Talladega in 1944, after three years of study. She took summer classes and passed examinations for advanced study. Jewel began her teaching career in 1945 as a teaching fellow in the biology department of New York University, where she received a master's degree, then a Ph.D. in cell physiology in 1950 at the age of twenty-six. In 1956, Dr. Cobb was appointed assistant professor in research surgery at New York University.

Dr. Cobb's area of specialty was pigment cell research, specifically, melanin. She was interested in melanin's ability to shield human skin from ultraviolet rays, and the possibility that it evolved in Africa. Her research involved skin cancer, known as melanoma.

By the 1960s African Americans with doctorates, who were discriminated against in previous years, were in high demand at traditionally white colleges and universities. Dr. Cobb held numerous positions as a professor and administrator in science. From 1960 to

THE RESEARCHER

In addition to her career as an educator, Dr. Cobb fulfilled her dream to do cancer research. Her research was conducted at the Harlem Hospital Cancer Research Foundation; the University of Illinois Medical School, where she instituted its tissue culture research lab; New York University–Bellevue Hospital Medical Center, where she established the tissue culture research laboratory; and Sarah Lawrence College. Dr. Cobb's research on cells and their relationship to skin cancer provided significant data to other researchers in their efforts to diagnose, treat, and find cures for cancer.

✦ **Data** is factual information, such as measurements, used for research.

✦ **Radiology** is the science of high-energy radiation, such as X rays.

1969, she was professor of biology at Sarah Lawrence College. In 1969, she accepted a position as professor of zoology at Connecticut College and was named dean of that college, a position she held until 1976.

Dr. Cobb believed that there should be more African American women and people of color in science. She was able to make a difference when she was appointed to the National Science Board, a policymaking body for the National Science Foundation. In 1976, Dr. Cobb became dean of Rutgers University's Douglass College, the women's division of the university. In 1981, she moved on to the presidency of California State University in Fullerton, where she remained until 1990. In 1991, Dr. Cobb became principal investigator at the Southern California Engineering and Science ACCESS Center at California State University.

In 1993, she was presented with the National Science Foundation's Lifetime Achievement Award for Contributions to the Advancement of Women and Underrepresented Minorities. Her photograph hangs in the National Academy of Sciences in Washington, D.C., an honor for her contributions to science. Dr. Cobb is also the proud mother of a son, Roy Jonathan Cobb, a radiologist in New Jersey.

ANGELA D.
FERGUSON, M.D.

(B. 1925)

◆

Angela D. Ferguson was born in Washington, D.C., on February 15, 1925. She was one of eight children. Her father was a teacher at Samuel Armstrong School, a segregated school in Washington, D.C. As a child, Angela learned the importance of working and helping the family. Many African Americans were woefully underpaid and lived in poverty in the 1920s.

Although the Ferguson family suffered economically, they never considered themselves poor, believing that the greatest poverty was that of the spirit. Angela's parents taught her and her siblings at an early age to hold their heads high, respect others, become educated, and contribute to humankind. Her parents emphasized that education is the vehicle to a productive life and a buffer to discrimination and oppression.

Angela was a talented student in elementary school, always making the honor roll. She loved to read and her teachers frequently praised her. Angela always wanted to know more. In her classes, she was the first to raise her hand to answer or ask a question. Her teachers recognized that she was destined to become a leader.

Angela enrolled at Cardozo High School. She was reluctant to attend Armstrong since her father was a teacher there and she did not want to be under his scrutiny. Angela's chemistry teacher at Cardozo made science come alive. She learned that science is everywhere: in the home, school, and community. Angela graduated at the top of her class in 1941.

+ **Anatomy** is the study of the parts of an animal or plant, such as the skeleton.

+ **Physiology** is the study of the functions and activities of living things.

+ **Pediatrics** is the branch of medicine dealing with children.

After high school, she worked as a secretary, but quickly realized that her real interest was in medicine. She entered Howard University, only a few blocks from her home. During college, Angela became interested in anatomy and physiology. After completing her bachelor of science degree, she was accepted to Howard's School of Medicine. Few African American women were in medical school. She recognized that she had to be smarter than her male colleagues to get respect.

While a medical student, she worked on various wards of Freedmen's Hospital. Angela felt blessed to walk the halls of this hospital where great physicians such as Dr. Daniel Hale Williams, the first doctor to perform open heart surgery, walked. She was especially drawn to the many sick children. Her love and interest in them convinced her to enter a two-year training program in pediatrics.

After completing her residency and passing the required medical board examinations, Dr. Ferguson opened a private pediatrics practice in Washington. Little research existed about the health of African American children. Dr. Ferguson knew that the research based on children of European heritage was not always relevant to the needs of African American children. Especially lacking was research about sickle cell anemia, a disease that occurs primarily among African Americans.

Dr. Ferguson wanted to find some relief for her patients. She joined Dr. Ronald Scott in researching sickle cell anemia. Through their intensive research—the first of its kind—they were able to develop a method for detecting the disease in children. Dr. Ferguson studied hundreds of cases of sickle cell anemia and discovered the symptoms. She found that the blood of sickle cell anemia patients is much thicker and more acidic than the blood of healthy individuals. These findings provided an innovative way to diagnose the disease. Dr. Ferguson instituted the practice of giving each newborn African American child a blood test to detect the presence of sickle cell anemia. This hemoglobin test determines if a child has the trait or a variant of sickle cell disease. Today, some forty states require testing of newborns for sickle cell disease.

Dr. Ferguson discovered ways to reduce the stress in sickle cell anemia patients when undergoing surgery. They were given extra oxygen after coming out of the anesthesia. For five-year-olds, she found that drinking extra water with a small amount of baking soda daily could give relief from severe symptoms.

AN URGENT CHALLENGE

Sickle cell anemia causes the red blood cells to function improperly. Healthy red blood cells are donut shaped, but the blood cells of sickle cell anemia patients are in a sickle shape, preventing the easy flow of blood in the veins and arteries. The misshapen cells can get stuck in the small blood vessels, stopping the flow of blood and oxygen. For decades, this problem has fascinated and mystified researchers.

There is still no cure for sickle cell disease. However, scientists have made advancements in easing the crises associated with the illness. Today, pioneering scientists such as Dr. Angela Ferguson are investigating ways to prevent a crisis from occurring at all, including blood transfusions and bone marrow transplants.

Dr. Ferguson was selected to oversee the massive construction of the Howard University Hospital. Completed in 1975, it is a 500-bed teaching hospital. In 1979, Dr. Ferguson was named Howard's associate vice president for health affairs. She retired from Howard in 1990.

REATHA CLARK
KING, Ph.D.
(B. 1938)

✦

Dr. Reatha Clark King, like other African American women inventors and scientists, never let the color of her skin define her as a person or limit her aspirations.

Reatha was born in the small town of Pavo, Georgia, on April 11, 1938. She was the second of three daughters born to Willie and Ola Watts Campbell Clark. Ola had a third-grade education and Willie was illiterate. They worked the land.

Reatha started grade school in 1942 at the one-room schoolhouse of Mt. Zion Baptist Church. Florence Frazier, one of Reatha's teachers, was a great influence. King recalls, "My older sister and I learned very quickly everything that Miss Frazier exposed us to. This became a pattern for the rest of our school years. Miss Frazier was a role model. I never wondered if I could succeed in a subject. It was only a question of whether I wanted to study the subject."[1]

In small, Southern towns, African American children had little formal education because they were frequently taken out of school to

work in the fields. Many of the schools for African Americans operated on a split-session system, meaning that children attended school only when they were not needed to plant and gather crops. Thus, Reatha did not know for sure if she would be able to stay in school.

One day, Reatha's father left Pavo to work on vegetable and sugarcane farms in Belle Glade, Florida. Soon afterward, Reatha's mother went north, seeking higher pay. Reatha moved in with her widowed grandmother, Mamie Watts, in Merrillville, a town near Pavo. Reatha walked miles along the Georgia dirt roads to church activities back in Pavo.

Although Reatha's grandmother was illiterate, it did not stop her from owning and caring for her own home and five acres of land. She was the epitome of strength. King recalls, "My grandmother left numerous impressions on me, but these words had special impact: 'If something is worth doing, it is worth doing right.'"[2]

After Reatha's mother returned from the North, Reatha and her sister lived in several different communities as their mother sought better work. Mrs. Clark was accustomed to working long hours to provide for her children. She found employment as a domestic, working more than sixty hours a week and rarely bringing home more than $20 for the week. To supplement her income, the girls would pick cotton, which was hard work with low pay.

But Reatha never stopped striving to learn. She stayed in school no matter how hard it was for her to work in the fields and study, too. Her favorite subjects were mathematics and science. She also loved to read. When she graduated from Moultrie High School for Negro Youth, she was valedictorian of her class.

In September 1954, Reatha entered Clark College. She supplemented her expenses by working in the registrar's office, earning 35 cents an hour. Reatha recalls:

Lack of money was the most painful memory of my undergraduate years. Paying for books, tuition, room and board, and miscellaneous expenses was difficult, even with a $250 tuition scholarship and a job. My mother was earning $18 per week with two daughters in college. These experiences taught me about the value of financial aid, and the kind of stress that students who lack funds experience.[3]

Reatha planned to major in home economics and return home to teach in her local high school. After her first chemistry course, her plans changed. Her chemistry teacher, Alfred Spriggs, recognized her special abilities and became her mentor. She soon decided to pursue a degree in chemistry. With the help of Dr. Spriggs, Reatha saw that she could excel in science.

Reatha Clark graduated with highest honors from Clark College in 1958. She was awarded the prestigious Woodrow Wilson Fellowship for graduate study from 1958 to 1960. She attended the University of Chicago for graduate school and earned her master's degree in chemistry. Clark received a National Medical Fellowship to pursue her Ph.D. in physical chemistry. This allowed her to support herself while pursuing her degree instead of depending on her mother's meager income.

While in graduate school, Reatha met N. Judge King Jr., a native of Birmingham, Alabama, and a graduate of Morehouse College. They married in December 1961. The first year of their marriage was a commuter marriage as Reatha completed her studies in Chicago and Judge attended graduate school in Atlanta. In December 1962, at age twenty-five, King was awarded a Ph.D. in chemistry.

After graduation, Dr. King searched for a job. Despite her excellent education and achievement, she faced discrimination and was not offered a suitable position. She remembered her mother's advice to always be persistent and never give up. In January 1963, Dr. King was hired by the National Bureau of Standards (NBS), a federal agency.

The Bureau of Standards recognized Dr. King's talent and assigned her to investigate the heat formed from gaseous fluoride compounds. This project was important to the success of the space program of the National Aeronautics and Space Administration (NASA). Two research teams had already failed. After three years of methodical investigation, Dr. King and her team were successful. Their achievements were published in numerous national and international journals.

Dr. King's two children, Jay and Scott, were born in 1965 and 1968.

After working at the Bureau of Standards for five years, Dr. King moved on to the chemistry faculty at York College of the City University of New York, in Jamaica, Queens, from 1968 to 1977. She also served as associate dean of natural science and mathematics and dean of academic affairs.

While working at York College, this energetic scientist found time to earn a master's of business administration (MBA) at Columbia University Graduate School of Business in 1977. That same year, Dr. King was named president of Metropolitan State University in St. Paul, Minnesota, becoming one of the few African American presidents of a major college or university. In 1988, she accepted a position as president and executive director of the General Mills Foundation, overseeing the awarding of more than $16 million in grants to worthy organizations and groups.

PERSISTENCE PAYS

PATRICIA COWINGS

As a child, scientist-astronaut Patricia Cowings, like Reatha King, followed her parents' admonition that anyone can learn and can achieve whatever they set out to do. As a result, Dr. Cowings was able to make her mark in space exploration. As the first African American woman to receive scientist-astronaut training, she conducted experiments on board the space shuttle. Dr. Cowings measured changes in bodily responses such as heart rate, sweating, and respiratory rate during motion sickness tests. One day, her research could help patients with brain disorders such as Parkinson's disease, or could help the military to improve pilot performance.

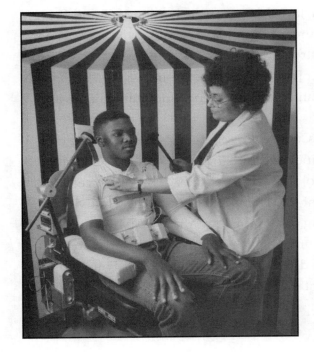

Patricia Cowings.

BETTY WRIGHT
HARRIS, PH.D

(B. 1940)

✦

Betty Wright grew up on two farms in northeast Louisiana, but her family came from a world away. She was the seventh of twelve children born to Henry Hudson "Jake" Wright and Legertha Evelyn Thompson Wright. Betty's mother grew up in Kenya and her father is Cherokee Indian.

According to Dr. Harris, "Until age twelve, I lived on a plantation with my family. We farmed and the owner charged us one-quarter of our profits. However, my parents would not let us shop at the local store or buy things on credit from the owners."[1] The Wrights were determined to rise above the poor conditions of others in the area. They became successful farmers, growing cotton, corn, sugarcane, potatoes, and a variety of vegetables. They supplemented their income by raising farm animals. Mr. Wright was a good businessman, encouraging his sons to learn skills such as carpentry and toolmaking. They made furniture from the dense forests that surrounded their land and tools such as cane knives. The Wright children learned much from the industry, persistence, and hard work of their parents.

84

Betty was instantly recognized in school for her abilities. She fell in love with reading and mathematics, and spent her leisure time reading and dreaming of faraway places. Betty showed a special interest in science at an early age. Her teachers often spoke of her as having a creative mind.

By the time Betty was in ninth grade, the Wrights bought land and built a five-bedroom house on it. The home was on the borderline of two school districts and Betty got to choose her school system. She chose Columbia, Louisiana. "It had an excellent high school, several times better than its 'white' counterpart, Harris shares.

Betty attended Union Central High School and was encouraged to pursue science as a career. She enrolled at Southern University at age sixteen, a historically black college in Baton Rouge, Louisiana, and received a bachelor of science degree at age nineteen. She continued her education at Atlanta University, where she received a master's degree.

After graduating from Atlanta University, Betty worked at Mississippi Valley State College, now Mississippi Valley State University (MVSU), a historically black college in Itta Bena, Mississippi. While teaching at MVSU was a great experience for her, she wanted to leave the classroom and get involved in research.

Along the way, she married, divorced, and had four children. Yet

A DETERMINED SPIRIT

Dr. Harris says, "It has been an exciting, fascinating, rewarding, and sometimes very challenging career."[2] She attributes her success to the many wonderful people who supported her and kept her strong, as well as to those who made her life totally miserable at times, because they helped to keep her focused. A determined person must always find a lesson in both positive and negative experiences.

she kept reaching higher. She chose the University of New Mexico to work on a Ph.D. Betty received a Ph.D. in chemistry in 1975.

Dr. Harris worked as a chemist with the Los Alamos National Laboratory in New Mexico, which is operated by the University of California for the United States Department of Energy. Dr. Harris has worked for more than twenty years researching and finding new discoveries in explosives and nuclear weapons. She began experimenting to find a way to spot test for an explosive called triamino trinitrobenzene (TATB). Her efforts paid off on November 29, 1984, when she applied for a patent for a spot test for 1,3,5 triamino-2,4,6-trinitrobenzene. Since Dr. Harris was an employee of Los Alamos National Laboratory, the patent was assigned to the United States Department of Energy.

This invention provided the military and private businesses with an effective way to test materials on the spot to determine if explosives were present. TATB is like synthetic sand. It is difficult to dissolve it in any medium. Therefore, it not easy to test for it. But Dr. Harris developed an extrasensitive process that dissolved enough of the TATB to give a good confirmation test.

In her patent application, Dr. Harris wrote about the importance of her invention:

> Among the benefits and advantages of the subject invention are the ability to perform sensitive, simple and specific tests for TATB content and the identification of this explosive in its pure form. It is an inexpensive test that can be used in the field or in the laboratory. If there is a partial detonation or an explosion and the materials are scattered, then this test solution can help determine how widespread the contamination has become.[3]

Over the years, Dr. Harris received numerous awards including New Mexico Governor's Trailblazers Award; the Toastmasters Award; and the 1999 Dr. Martin Luther King, Jr. Citizenship Award. In addition, she found time to be the committee chair for several professional and community organizations and to mentor youth interested in careers in science and technology.

Dr. Harris designed an experiment for and participated in the making of a CD ROM entitled *Telling Our Stories: Women in Science* (for ages ten and up). This CD ROM was published by McLean Media. It can be viewed at http://www.storyline.com.

Dr. Harris wants to encourage parent and teachers, too:

> We must start early, provide the experiences, be consistent, and work with an end goal in mind. We must be the best that we can as parents and teachers and stay actively involved. Hold our families to high educational standards and expectations. Sit down and eat some meals together and just talk to each other. Then, we must get technical with computers and other technologies in the home.[4]

Dr. Harris has turned her attention to the cleanup of weapons sites. To determine which areas were contaminated, she analyzed soil and water samples. Her results guided decisions about future uses of the Los Alamos facility. Today, Dr. Harris works for an African American–owned company named Columbia Services Group, Inc., which provides support to the Department of Energy (DOE).

JUST DO IT

Dr. Harris has some advice for young people who are interested in pursuing a career in science: "I say, do it. It is worth the effort. The pursuit will sometimes be difficult. You may not have the money, the time, the basic life necessities, or even the results on your experiments that advisors want. But get the degree(s). For you, the world will open up. The view, the opportunities, the salary will all be beautiful."

PATRICIA
BATH, M.D.

(B. 1942)

✦

Patricia Bath always liked to solve problems. By the time she was in high school, everyone in her New York neighborhood of Harlem could see that she was a gifted student in science and mathematics. Remembering the teachings of her parents, "Never settle for less than your best," Patricia studied hard and earned a spot in advanced classes in these subjects. Patricia's teachers recognized her talents and encouraged her to pursue a career in science.

Patricia attended New York's Charles Evans Hughes High School. Her first biology course excited her interest in science. She spent many hours helping in the lab to learn more about biology. This dedication was also evident in the many science awards she received. In 1959, Patricia's excellence paid off when she was selected for a National Science Foundation summer program for high school students at Yeshiva University.

After high school, Patricia found a job working at Yeshiva University and Harlem Hospital on a cancer research team. She was mentored by Rabbi Moses D. Tendler and Dr. Robert O. Bernard,

89

cancer researchers. Patricia was a gifted researcher. She collected and analyzed experimental data, developed a hypothesis, and developed a mathematic equation to predict cancer cell growth. She enjoyed the work and thrived on the daily challenges. Her contribution to the research team was so helpful that Patricia was credited as one of the co-authors on a research report read at the Fifth Annual International Congress on Nutrition in Washington, D.C., on September 2, 1960. At age seventeen, Patricia felt certain about her future: She would go to college and pursue a degree in medicine.

Patricia entered Hunter College in New York City. Not surprisingly, she was always on the dean's list. In 1964, Patricia received a bachelor of arts degree in chemistry with highest honors. She went on to Howard University Medical School. There she received numerous scholarships and awards, including the National Institute of Health Fellowship and the National Institute of Mental Health Fellowship in 1965.

Howard University was a great experience for Patricia. It was the first time she was exposed to black professors. She found especially concerned, committed mentors in Dr. LaSalle D. Lefall, Jr., and Dr. Lois A. Young, both eminent professors.

While attending medical school, Patricia spent the summer of 1967 on a research project concerning children's health in Yugoslavia. This experience heightened her interest in international medicine. Her interest in helping disadvantaged people motivated her to spend many hours as the medical coordinator for the Poor People's Campaign that marched in Washington, D.C., for economic rights in 1968.

Patricia received her medical degree in 1968. After medical school, she trained in ophthalmology and worked as an assistant of surgery at many New York hospitals. After 1973, Dr. Bath went to California, where she continued her training in ophthalmology. In 1977, Dr. Bath went to

✦ **Ophthalmology** is the study of the human eye.

Nigeria, in Africa, where she was chief of ophthalmology at Mercy Hospital. She served on the White House Counsel for National and International Blindness Prevention Program from 1977 to 1978.

In 1978, Dr. Bath founded the American Institute for Prevention of Blindness. Intrigued by what she was beginning to read about laser treatments for eye diseases, Dr. Bath quickly located experts in the field. She went all the way to Berlin University in Germany. Based on what she learned in Germany, she designed a model of a laser instrument for removing cataracts. Cataracts are a condition affecting the eye, where the lens becomes dark, causing partial or total blindness. Dr. Bath applied for a patent for her instrument and on May 17, 1988, she became the first African American female doctor to receive a patent for a medical invention.

✦ A **model** is an example or pattern of something to be made.

Dr. Bath's invention changed eye surgery. The development of cataracts is normal as people grow older. Sometimes, eye injuries can also cause cataracts. The only treatment is surgery. During surgery, Dr. Bath's invention, known as the laserphacoprobe, produces a powerful, concentrated beam of light that breaks up and virtually destroys the cataract. It is used throughout the world. Dr. Bath kept improving her invention and now has four patents to her credit: apparatus for ablating and removing cataract lenses, issued on May 17, 1988; method and apparatus for ablating and removing cataract lenses, issued December 1, 1998; laser apparatus for surgery of cataractous lenses, issued July 6, 1999; and pulsed ultrasound method for fragmenting/emulsifying and removing cataractous lenses, issued July 4, 2000. Her work in ophthalmology has saved the vision of many people. Dr. Bath continues to work in medicine at Howard University Hospital.

NOTABLE FIRSTS FOR AFRICAN AMERICAN WOMEN DOCTORS

- **Rebecca Lee Crumpler** was the first African American woman physician. In 1864, she graduated from the New England Female Medical College, which is now Boston University School of Medicine.

- **Verina M. Jones** was the first woman doctor in Mississippi. She graduated from the Woman's Medical College of Pennsylvania in 1888. Known today as the Medical College of Pennsylvania, it is open to male students. It continues its strong commitment to women in the medical profession.

- **Doris Shockley** was the first woman to earn a Ph.D. in pharmacology in the United States, in 1955.

  ◆ **Pharmacology** is the study of preparing and using medicines.

- **Edith Irby Jones** was the first woman president of the National Medical Association.

- **Renee Rosilind Jenkins** was the first African American president of the Society of Adolescent Medicine (1989–1990).

- **Roselyn Epps** was the first African American president of the American Medical Women's Association (1990).

- **Jocelyn Elders** was the first African American female U.S. Surgeon General.

THOMAS

(B . 1 9 4 3)

✦

Valerie Thomas never believed that science and mathematics were for boys only. When she was eight years old, she went to the public library in Baltimore and checked out her first book, *The Boy's First Book on Electronics.* The title did not stop her; that book was made for her. While most girls in the neighborhood were playing with dolls and jumping rope, Valerie was busy tinkering with radios. Some of her neighbors thought this was a strange pursuit for a girl, but her parents encouraged her.

Valerie was born on February 1, 1943, in Baltimore, Maryland. Her early fascination with electronics came from her father. One day, he showed Valerie how to take a radio apart, explaining the components and where they fit. She became good at repairing wiring and radio tubes. Those same neighbors who talked about her hobby would often stop by so that Valerie could fix their radios. Later, when

✦**Electronics** is the branch of physics that deals with the power of electricity.

✦**Components** are the parts or ingredients in a system, such as a motor.

televisions became popular, Valerie learned how pictures were transmitted electronically and soon could repair televisions.

From elementary school through high school, Valerie was at the top of her class. Her favorite subjects were science and mathematics. When she entered high school, she demonstrated special abilities in science and was challenged by her teachers to pursue this field. Often, Valerie would finish her work before her classmates. Teachers had to plan special activities just to keep her interested.

After high school, Valerie enrolled at Morgan State University in Baltimore, Maryland. She received a degree in physics with highest honors and was recruited by several companies, but Valerie decided to join the National Aeronautics and Space Administration (NASA). As a mathematician and data analyst, she worked on the development of the Landsat image processing system for more than ten years. Landsat was the first satellite to provide images from outer space. These images help us to understand our own planet. As an assistant program manager of Landsat, Thomas used space technology to help predict worldwide crop yields.

Even as an adult, Thomas was tinkering with electronics. On October 21, 1980, she received a patent on an illusion transmitter. The invention transmitted real images and works like a television transmitter. It sent signals through the air, just like a television, and produced three-dimensional images.

In the late 1980s, Thomas was project manager for the Space Physics Analysis Network (SPAN). SPAN is a computer network connecting thousands of research stations. Such a network enables scientists in the United States, South America, Canada, and Europe to communicate and collaborate on research.

The first electronics book that Thomas read may have been for boys, but she never allowed herself to be limited by what others thought.

IMAGINE THIS . . .

MARIE VAN BRITTAN BROWN

In 1969, Marie Van Brittan Brown of Jamaica, New York, patented a modern home security system using television surveillance. She received the patent jointly with Albert L. Brown. In the application filed by Brown and Brown on August 1, 1966, the invention is described as a home video and audio security system. Brown's security system included a picture of the person at the door on video and his or her voice on tape. The person inside could talk to the visitor without opening the door. A radio-controlled alarm alerted a guard, police officer, or watchperson at a security station.

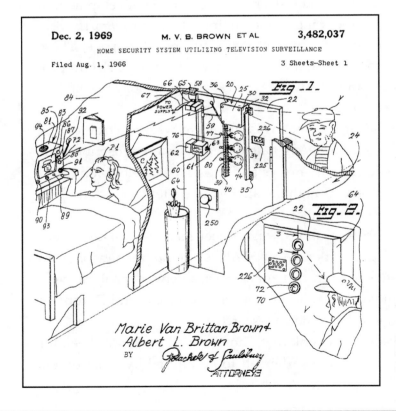

Marie Van Brittan Brown's home security system kept intruders out and the people inside safe.

SHIRLEY ANN

JACKSON, PH.D.

(B. 1946)

✦

As a child, Shirley Ann Jackson's nickname was the "Brain," and with good reason. She was born on August 5, 1946, in Washington, D.C., the second daughter of Beatrice and George Jackson. She grew up in a strong, close family that expected her to achieve. Her mother, a social worker, read biographies of famous African Americans to her. Her father always advised her to "aim for the stars so that you can reach the treetops." Always adventurous, Jackson collected live bumblebees, hornets, and wasps just for fun. Some of her neighbors thought it was unladylike to collect bugs and told her so, but Shirley didn't care.

Like a real scientist, Shirley took care of her specimens, placing them in old mayonnaise jars under the back porch. Shirley methodically adjusted their habitats, diets, and exposure to light and heat. She kept many notes on her observations. Shirley also studied molds and fungi around her home. Turning her curiosity into a science experiment, she

✦ A **specimen** is a specially chosen sample.

✦ A **habitat** is the place where a plant or animal naturally lives and grows.

investigated the effect of the environment on the growth of bacteria and won first place at a science fair. Dr. Jackson recalls, "From my perspective in those days, experimentation was like a good mystery novel, a tangible, unfolding narrative of what made nature click. In other words, it was a set of ideas with concrete, practical application."[1]

Shirley attended Roosevelt High School and took advanced mathematics, biology and chemistry classes. She also studied Latin for six years. Jackson graduated from Roosevelt High in 1964 as valedictorian of her class. A vice principal at Roosevelt suggested that Jackson apply to the prestigious Massachusetts Institute of Technology (MIT). She received an academic scholarship and became one of only fifteen African American students that year to enroll at MIT, and one of forty-three women in her freshman class of nine hundred; only one other was African American.

At first, college was difficult for Shirley. White students avoided eating with her in the cafeteria and did not invite her to join their study groups, so she spent many long hours studying alone. On one occasion, a group of men shouted racial epithets at her and one spit in her face. Shirley was undaunted: "It was important to not just focus on myself but rather to understand that I had a particular opportunity."[2] One professor suggested, "Colored girls should learn a trade." She became even more determined to become a physicist.

During the second semester, she was chosen to be a laboratory assistant. Other students began to ask her for tutoring. She no longer felt isolated and was confident she would succeed.

When Jackson received her bachelor of science degree in 1968, scholarship offers came in from Harvard University, the University of Chicago, and Brown University. She decided to remain at MIT for graduate studies. Her decision was an easy one when she learned that her advisor would be Dr. James Young, MIT's first tenured, or permanent, African American physics professor. Few African Americans were hired as science professors and even fewer were tenured at

THE MATHEMATICIAN

MARJORIE LEE BROWNE

Marjorie Lee Browne earned her doctorate in mathematics from the University of Michigan in 1949, becoming one of the first two African American women to earn a doctorate in mathematics. As professor of mathematics at North Carolina Central University, she encouraged a number of students to pursue a degree in mathematics. Nine of her students earned a doctorate in the mathematics sciences or related disciplines.

In 1960, Dr. Browne received a $60,000 grant from IBM to establish one of the first electronic digital computer centers at a predominantly African American university. She was one of the first African American females to serve on an advisory panel of the National Science Foundation.

Marjorie Lee Browne was one of the first African American women to earn a Ph.D. in mathematics.

predominantly white universities. Dr. Jackson received her Ph.D. at age twenty-six, becoming the first African American female in the country to receive a Ph.D. in physics.

According to Jackson, as a physicist she "tried to understand the interaction of the basic particles of matter. I worked in what was known as interacting physics, where one uses mathematics to study the 'forces' holding together the nucleus of an atom."

Dr. Jackson worked in several famous laboratories all over the world. After sixteen years of research, she was appointed professor of physics at Rutgers University. She has published more than a hundred scientific papers and has received countless awards. Along the way, she married another physicist, Dr. Morris Washington, and had a son, Alan, who entered Dartmouth College in Hanover, New Hampshire.

In 1995, Dr. Jackson became the first African American to head the Nuclear Regulatory Commission, which oversees nuclear power plants that provide more than 20 percent of the nation's electricity. She is the first African American president of Rensselaer Polytechnic Institute in New York, the nation's oldest university dedicated to science and engineering. Her students are mostly white males. Dr. Jackson wants to attract more women and minorities to the institution. Dr. Shirley Ann Jackson, who followed her father's advice to aim high, wants more women and minorities to follow her path and study science.

ALEXA
CANADY, M.D.
(B. 1950)

✦

Alexa Canady was one of four children born to Clinton Canady Jr., a Lansing, Michigan, dentist, and Hortense Golden Canady, a homemaker. Alexa's mother was the first African American elected to the Lansing school board. Born on November 7, 1950, Alexa was bright and inquisitive. Her parents encouraged her curiosity. Throughout her childhood, they made sure that Alexa and her siblings had lots of books, took trips to museums, saw plays, and traveled.

Alexa earned excellent grades in all of her classes. She astounded her teachers, who couldn't believe that a little African American girl achieved far above the white students. In second grade, a teacher refused to give Alexa the high grade she had earned. The school district investigated and discovered the teacher had indeed been unfair. The teacher was fired.

It was Alexa's first experience with racial discrimination. Even after the landmark U.S. Supreme Court Decision in *Brown vs. Board of Education*, which outlawed segregated public schools in 1954, many

American schools, both in the North and the South, remained segregated. Alexa's experience was not unusual.

The problem was at its worst in the Deep South. When nine African American students, known as the Little Rock Nine, were admitted to Little Rock's Central High School for the 1957–1958 school year, President Dwight D. Eisenhower had to order a thousand army paratroopers to Little Rock to protect the students. Daisy Bates, the president of the Arkansas chapter of the National Association for the Advancement of Colored People and a leading advocate of the students, escorted them safely to school until the crisis was resolved.

Alexa and her family read the newspaper about the Little Rock Nine and probably even watched the story unfold on television, inspired by the students' courage. Alexa wondered if she could be as brave. She graduated from high school with highest honors in 1967 and entered the University of Michigan (UM), where she received a bachelor of science degree. At Michigan, she was actively involved in the debate team and was a journalist for the student newspaper. When she enrolled at UM, she planned to become a theoretical mathematician. She then became convinced that mathematics was not her niche, explaining, "I had a crisis of confidence. I did okay, but I didn't like it as much as those guys liked it."[1]

✦ A **theoretical** explanation is one that scientists believe might be true.

✦ A **mathematician** studies the science of numbers.

Alexa entered medical school at Michigan and was an outstanding student. In 1975, she received her degree, in addition to a citation from the American Medical Women's Association. Alexa was ready to leave Michigan and decided to intern at the New Haven Hospital in Connecticut from 1974 to 1975.

After completing her internship, she was offered a special opportunity to do her residency at the University of Minnesota. Dr. Canady became the first African American to do a neurological residency

Eight of the Little Rock Nine.

there. She recalls, "When I got a residency in neurosurgery, I got it not because I'm smarter than somebody forty years ago, but because the politics were such that they needed a black woman and I was there and qualified."[2] From 1976 to 1981, Dr. Canady remained on the staff at the University of Minnesota. At the end of her residency, she became interested in pediatric neurosurgery. She made another move to Pennsylvania to work at the Children's Hospital of Philadelphia. In 1982, Dr. Canady moved back home to Michigan to work in Detroit

A PERFECT FIT

People often do not know what they want to be, even when they become adults. Sometimes they change jobs or change majors in college. Dr. Canady was no different. She found she did not love mathematics, but her switch to medicine was not an overnight decision. During the summer, when she needed money for a car for her job on the newspaper, her brother, Michael, who was also a student at the University of Michigan, told Alexa about a minority health care program that required her to work from 8 A.M. to 5 P.M. Her job on the newspaper started at 5 P.M., so it was a perfect fit. Alexa began working with Art Bloom, a pediatrician and geneticist, and she fell in love with the work. At the end of the summer, Alexa switched her interest from mathematics to science. She took a class in neurology and loved it. She'd found the perfect career for her.

- ✦ A **pediatrician** is a doctor who specializes in treating children.
- ✦ A **geneticist** studies the branch of biology that deals with inherited traits.
- ✦ **Neurology** is the study of the nervous system.

at Henry Ford Hospital as an instructor of neurosurgery. In 1983, she moved to another hospital in Detroit, the nationally recognized Children's Hospital of Michigan.

Dr. Canady was named teacher of the year at Children's Hospital in 1984. That same year, the American Board of Neurological Surgery certified her. In 1985, Dr. Canady joined Wayne State University's School of Medicine as a clinical instructor. By 1991, she was vice chairman of the department of neurosurgery.

Today, Dr. Canady is chief of neurosurgery at Children's Hospital in Detroit, Michigan. Her days are filled with working, mentoring students, and making speeches throughout the country. In 1995, Dr.

Canady and Dr. Olivier DeLalanda, a Paris neurosurgeon, performed a hemispherotomy, the first such operation in Michigan, on Cayla Babish. The left side of Cayla's brain was abnormally large. This caused epilepsy, the bursts of electrical activity that result in seizures. Essentially, Cayla's brain was rewired to prevent seizures.

Dr. Alexa Canady prepares for surgery.

SHARON J.
BARNES

(B. 1955)

✦

Sharon J. Barnes belongs to the second generation of college grad-
uates in her family. She was born on November 28, 1955, in Beaumont,
Texas, to Selna and William Jefferson McDonald, both native Texans.
Sharon's mother attended Texas Southern University and her father
attended Prairie View A&M University. Her parents admonished her
to work hard and never stop until a task was completed.

Sharon recalls that her mother instilled a can-do spirit in her and
her two sisters and brother. She loved school and filled her days with
student activities and reading. Mr. McDonald exposed his children to
travel, constantly reminding them that the world extended far beyond
their neighborhood.

During high school, Sharon was always busy, involved in both
school and church. All along, Sharon had mentors who encouraged
her to pursue a career in science, for instance, the family physician,
Dr. W. J. Postaske, and her high school biology teacher, Sherry
Woodard, a registered nurse.

Sharon was convinced that she would attend college and recalls

that in her family "It was never *if* you go to college, it was *when* you go to college."[1] She received three scholarships.

Sharon was accepted to Baylor University (BU) in Waco, Texas. During college, she interned at the Baptist Hospital of Southeast Texas in the medical technology program. Sharon received a bachelor of science degree in biochemistry and clinical laboratory science. In 1979, she was certified as a medical technologist and worked at the Community Hospital of Brazosport in Texas until 1986. She liked her job, but was interested in becoming a full-time chemist.

In 1987, Sharon found a job as a chemist with Dow Chemical, the fifth largest company in the world. She has been a clinical laboratory director, an environmental chemist, and the global human resources manager, overseeing more than 5,600 employees.

Barnes was a member of a team of five, including one other African American, who invented the process and apparatus for contactless measurement of sample temperature. Barnes and her co-inventors found a way to test the temperature of a laboratory sample without having to touch it. This can make the results more accurate, because there is less chance of contamination.

ALWAYS ASK CHALLENGING QUESTIONS

Barnes has some advice for future scientists:

Future scientists should always ask challenging questions and look for a better way to do just about anything. Always seek knowledge and understanding for yourself. Just don't take someone's word, but do your homework. Always be willing to work hard, have faith, and trust in yourself that you can make a positive difference.

With the can-do spirit of her childhood, Barnes has always been active in her community and believes in giving back. Currently, she is mayor pro-tem of the city of Lake Jackson, Texas, a community of 25,000 people. She has also served as a city council member. Along the way, Sharon married Ronald Barnes, vice principal of Brazoswood High School. They are the proud parents of twins, Ronnie and Amber.

Barnes still works for the Dow Chemical Company in Texas.

MAE
JEMISON, M.D.

(B. 1956)

✦

As a little girl, Mae Jemison wondered if there were aliens in outer space and worried that the aliens would bump into an American spacecraft full of men and think that all humans looked like these guys. Mae was only eight years old when the first woman, Valentina Tereshkova, went into space. It was her early affirmation that women could also go into space.

Mae Jemison was born in Decatur, Alabama, on October 17, 1956. Her father, Charlie, was a maintenance supervisor, and her mother, Dorothy Green, taught English and math. At age three, Mae moved to Chicago with her family. Mae's uncle encouraged her to study astronomy, anthropology, evolution, and archaeology. Young Mae was curious about the world around her and asked many questions.

Her parents, teachers, and mentors knew that Mae was destined to achieve greatness. Mae always considered her parents her best role models, saying, "They demanded and demonstrated that one should seek to understand the world around them, and always be open to learning." Mae says, "The joy of my life as a young child came from

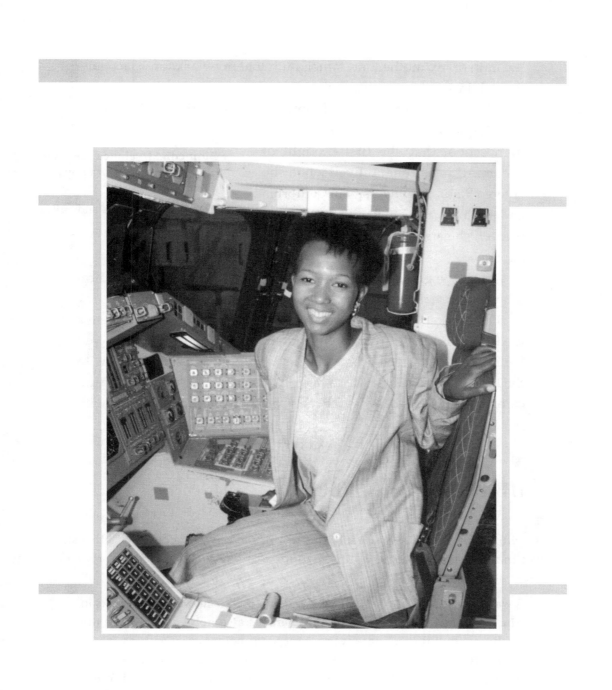

the faith of my mother and father, faith that my black forebears gave their children."[1]

Mae became interested in biomedical engineering while attending Morgan Park High School. It was in high school that she first thought of becoming an astronaut. Even when she entered Stanford University in California and became involved with dance and theater, she still wanted to be an astronaut.

+ **Biomedical science** involves biology, medicine, and physical science.

+ An **engineer** designs and builds mechanical devices.

When she graduated from Stanford in 1977, Mae entered medical school at Cornell University.

Dr. Jemison's interest in international medicine took her to Kenya in 1979. In 1981, she graduated from medical school and completed her internship the next year. Dr. Jemison worked as a staff doctor with the Peace Corps in West Africa from 1983 to 1985. She managed health care for the U.S. Embassy and Peace Corp personnel and worked with

THE WORLD TRAVELER

Before Mae Jemison went out of this world, she traveled all over it. When she was in medical school, she volunteered for a summer in a Cambodian refugee camp in Thailand.

> I was a fourth-year medical student and I helped to take care of patients in the emergency room of the refugee camp. I also helped to oversee the asthma clinic there. There was a very high incidence of asthma in the camp. It was one of the best experiences of my life because I learned so much about myself, as I viewed the world from a very different perspective.[2]

the National Institutes of Health and the Centers for Disease Control. Dr. Jemison also worked on several research projects, including the development of a hepatitis B vaccine.

However, Dr. Jemison still wanted to be an astronaut, and in 1986 she applied to the National Aeronautics and Space Administration's training program. That same year, the space shuttle *Challenger* exploded, causing NASA to suspend their acceptance of applications. Dr. Jemison reapplied in October 1987 and was one of fifteen candidates selected from two thousand applicants. After completing one

Education and a belief in herself prepared Mae C. Jemison to be the first African American woman in space.

year of training in August 1988, she qualified to be a mission specialist. Dr. Jemison's long-awaited space flight came in 1992 on the space shuttle *Endeavor.* She became the first African American woman in space.

On the space shuttle, Dr. Jemison took a poster of dancer/choreographer Judith Jemison performing *Cry,* a dance dedicated to the lives of African American women. During the weeklong flight, Dr. Jemison researched various topics including how to prevent motion sickness with positive thinking. For Dr. Jemison, the trip confirmed that she was a part of the world. She shares in her QuestChat, "It was assuring to think/feel that I belonged anywhere in this universe, whether it was on Earth and the River Nile, or in a star system 10,000 light-years away."

In 1993, Dr. Jemison left NASA to work on projects related to the environment, women and minorities. She has co-sponsored an international science camp for kids between twelve and sixteen years of age. The camp emphasizes critical thinking and experiential learning. Dr. Jemison is currently a professor of environmental studies at Dartmouth College in Hanover, New Hampshire.

When asked about being selected the first African American woman in space, she states, "I'm very aware of the fact that I'm not the first woman of color, the first African American woman, who had the skills, the talent, the desire to be an astronaut. I know that I happen to be the first one that NASA selected."

Ursula
BURNS

(B. 1958)

Growing up on New York's Lower East Side, Ursula Burns faced a discouraging problem: Sometimes her family was short of food. Her single mother made sacrifices to make sure that Ursula would never go hungry. But times were hard.

In elementary school, Ursula worked on keeping a positive attitude. She enjoyed reading, doing math, and experimenting with science projects. Ursula attended a Catholic high school where the teachers encouraged girls to become secretaries, nurses, or teachers. Always a leader, Ursula organized the school's Black Student Union, which worried the teachers. They punished her for planning and participating in marches and demonstrations.

Ursula had dreams far beyond her teachers' imaginations. She read college manuals and bulletins from cover to cover. She knew that an education would help her achieve all of her goals. Ursula planned ahead for her future. She remembered the poverty she knew as a child and vowed to leave it behind. In the summer, she worked as an intern

at the Xerox Corporation. Almost every day, she thought about what she wanted to do when she grew up.

When the time came, Ursula chose engineering because it was a high-paying field that fit her technical talents. She had learned about engineering careers at Xerox.

Her mother was unable to pay her college expenses, but Ursula hoped that since she was a good student, she would get a scholarship to attend college. She got her scholarship and enrolled in the Polytechnic Institute of New York. She majored in math and engineering, and received a bachelor of science degree in 1980. Xerox was recruiting African American students and she joined the company. With financial aid from Xerox, she received a master's degree in engineering from Columbia University in 1981.

Remaining at Xerox, Burns quickly rose in the ranks. Her mentor, Wayland Hicks, after observing how talented she was, took her on as his executive assistant. Hicks was impressed with her work habits and drive. Burns was promoted six times in seven years.

Xerox would need her intelligence and engineering talent very soon. By October 1997, the company had spent six years and nearly half a billion dollars developing a new digital copier. This copier didn't just copy; it also printed, scanned, and faxed. To solve unexpected problems with this new machine, Xerox called in Ursula Burns. Burns began to figure out the problems. She presented her ideas and solutions to the Xerox executives. She fixed last-minute design flaws and decreased the manufacturing time of the copier from nine hours to three hours. This machine became one of Xerox's best-sellers.

Xerox appointed Burns head of worldwide manufacturing. Burns became the highest-ranking African American woman at Xerox. She was not content to let this be her last achievement, however. Burns is currently senior vice president for Corporate Strategic Services at Xerox Corporation. She is the first woman to be named to this executive position. Burns holds several appointments including member of the executive board for the Hunt Corporation in Philadelphia, Pennsylvania, and Lincoln Electric Corporation in Cleveland, Ohio; member of the board of directors for FIRST, Allendale Columbia School Board, Boy Scouts of America, and the University of Rochester Medical School. She is also a member of the Board of Trustees of Polytechnic University.

APRILLE JOY ERICSSON
JACKSON, Ph.D.

(B. 1963)

✦

Aprille Joy Ericsson Jackson became interested in science in first grade when she saw the U.S. mission to the moon. She says it wasn't until high school that she realized, "I just loved to figure out how things work and move and I loved putting things together."

Aprille was born on April 1, 1963, in Brooklyn, New York to Corrinne Elaine Breedy and Hank Anthony Ericsson. She grew up in a strong, close-knit family that placed an emphasis on education. She was encouraged by her family to achieve. Her greatest motivator was her mom, who frequently told her, "You can be anything you want to be." Grandpa Ericsson was a train engineer and would often take Aprille to his job. Always curious and intelligent, she was the only African American student enrolled in the gifted and talented program at her junior high school, where she excelled in mathematics and science.

Aprille was a well-rounded student and athlete. She was a member of the girls' basketball team, the science club, the honors club, and lead clarinet in the band. In junior high school, she won second place in the science fair and scored high on all of her state and citywide

examinations. With these outstanding scores, she was guaranteed admission to several of the highly rated high schools.

Aprille was accepted to all of New York's technical high schools: the Bronx School of Science, Stuyvesant, and Brooklyn Technical. But instead of attending one of these schools, she accepted a full scholarship to attend the Cambridge School of Weston, Massachusetts, and was happy to join her grandparents in Cambridge, Massachusetts. Her grandfather was an engineer for the Sheraton Commander Hotel in Cambridge. He introduced Aprille to many challenges. She says, "He would get me up on the scaffold to paint the house, fix the gutters, repair, paint or wallpaper anything in the house."

In high school, Aprille was always on the honor roll, graduating at the top of her class. She received a scholarship to Massachusetts Institute of Technology (MIT). While attending MIT, Aprille became involved in several projects about manned space flight. She knew that one day she would apply for NASA's astronaut program. Aprille received a bachelor of science degree in aeronautical/astronautical engineering in June 1986.

That same year, a NASA space shuttle exploded, making jobs at NASA scarce. Aprille was encouraged by her best friend to go to graduate school at Howard University in Washington, D.C. At Howard, she obtained a master's of engineering degree in May 1990 and a Ph.D. in mechanical engineering in August 1995.

During the summers while working on her Ph.D., she traveled to Germany, Canada, England, and throughout the United States to present research papers.

Dr. Ericsson Jackson now works as an aerospace engineer at the NASA Goddard Space Flight Center in the Guidance, Navigation and Control Center. She says that the most challenging part of her job is understanding how all the components of a spacecraft work together. To understand how spacecrafts work, she conducts simulations. They

SCHOOLS OF ENGINEERING AT HISTORICALLY BLACK COLLEGES AND UNIVERSITIES

Several historically black colleges and universities have schools of engineering:

Florida A&M, Tallahassee, Florida
Hampton University, Hampton, Virginia
Howard University, Washington, D.C.
Morgan State University, Baltimore, Maryland
North Carolina A&T State University, Greensboro, North Carolina
Prairie View A&M University, Prairie View, Texas
Southern University, Baton Rouge, Louisiana
Tennessee State University, Nashville, Tennessee
Tuskegee University, Tuskegee, Alabama

allow her to see what changes should be made to spacecraft construction and design.

Dr. Ericsson Jackson teaches at Howard University in the mechanical engineering department. She is also an adjunct professor in the mathematics department at Bowie State University in Bowie, Maryland.

Dr. Ericsson Jackson has helped to spur the interest of minorities and females in mathematics, science and engineering. She believes that without diversity in all fields the United States will not remain technically competitive. A mentor may be the single most important weapon a young engineering student can have. She has conducted Women of NASA Online Interactive Sessions where she can talk with students worldwide. Individuals can access NASA's schedule of events by visiting http://quest.arc.nasa.gov/common/events.

Dr. Ericsson Jackson's
Advice to Young Scientists

I feel it is important to create an early mathematical and/or scientific interest in young people and maintain it throughout their later years; therefore, I work with all student age groups." She encourages all students to read every day, to turn off the TV more often, to work hard, but also to play hard. "Explore the realms of science, for it is so intriguing.[1]

Dannellia Gladden
GREEN, Ph.D.

(B. 1966)

✦

Dr. Dannellia Gladden Green was always a high achiever, even at J. E. B. Stuart Elementary School in Richmond, Virginia. Her parents would not have it any other way.

Her mother was a particularly strong influence in her life. Dannellia recalls, "I saw my mother start her own business, and to this day, she is still an owner-operator working very hard. I have never known her to say 'I can't bear it, or I can't do it.' That has been a real encouragement to me."

Young Dannellia Gladden attended Henderson Middle School in Richmond, Virginia, where she was a serious student and found science and mathematics exciting. She enrolled at Henrico High School in Richmond, Virginia. Her senior year was spent at Smith High School in Greensboro, North Carolina.

As a high school student, Dannellia always gave her best. She played basketball, volleyball, ran track, and participated in the literary arts club and debate team. While she enjoyed all of these activities, her focus was on preparing for college. Dannellia's caring teachers gave her

127

considerable support, instilling discipline and expecting excellence. She, in turn, always earned high test scores. "I had strong women teachers who pushed me toward science," she recalls. "They encouraged me to participate in summer collegiate programs while in high school, which helped me decide to pursue a career in engineering."[1]

Dannellia graduated at the top of her high school class. She entered North Carolina A&T State University, and graduated summa cum laude with a bachelor of science degree in 1988. Following her mother's example of always working hard, Dannellia pressed on to graduate school. She entered Massachusetts Institute of Technology (MIT). "I had a great time at MIT," she recalls. "Faculty was supportive, students were welcoming, and the administration had the proper hooks in place for one to succeed."[2]

After completing her master's degree in 1991, Dannellia joined Texas Instruments Company as an engineer in 1991. She returned to her roots in North Carolina to pursue a Ph.D. in electronic materials at North Carolina State University (NCSU) in 1993 and received the degree in 1996.

Once again, she approached school with a determination to do her best. Dannellia says, "I've never looked at something and identified

"KNOW THAT YOU KNOW"

Focus on the fundamentals and you will have a solid foundation. Know that you know when you know that you know; this will serve you well when faced with challenging issues. When striving to answer a question or find the root cause of a phenomenon, answer *Why* at least five times. No matter how intelligent you think you are, recognize that there is a power much greater than us all and acknowledge our creator in all things.[3]

—*Dannellia Gladden Green*

it as a barrier or thought that I did not have what it took to get a job done. When you want to accomplish a goal, you must know that it is possible. If you spend any amount of time thinking about why it can't be done, then you've given into a distraction that will only serve to prolong things."[4]

In 1996, Dr. Gladden Green returned to Texas Instruments full time. She has written and published many articles and has frequently served on numerous panels for engineering organizations. A wife and mother of three young children, Dr. Gladden Green teaches them that they can overcome any barriers and succeed.

Dr. Gladden Green was fortunate to have several mentors and she does her own mentoring of college students. She assists women from her alma maters by counseling them about graduate school choices and their careers.

DR. GLADDEN GREEN'S ADVICE TO TEACHERS

Dr. Gladden Green suggests, "Teachers need to continue to encourage creativity in the classroom. The earlier students are introduced to the concepts of science from a fun perspective, the increased likelihood that they will not be intimidated by it later."[5] According to her, teachers need to have challenging projects, bright ideas contests, and patentable proposal contests. These are just a few things that will encourage individual and group contributions.

CHAVONDA J. JACOBS
YOUNG, PH.D.
(B. 1967)

✦

Chavonda was born on July 16, 1967, in Augusta, Georgia. She was raised by her mother, Clide Mack Coppin. Throughout her childhood, Chavonda was active in church. At Barton Chapel Elementary School, she was a student leader. Academically talented, Chavonda also participated in track and field and the Girl Scouts.

At Glenn Hills High School, Chavonda was enrolled in a program to encourage minorities in science and mathematics. She decided to concentrate on engineering. Chavonda was always on the honor roll and became a member of the National Honor Society. She was a star athlete in track and field, receiving awards as the High School All-American Track Athlete and the Most Valuable Track Athlete.

Chavonda graduated from Hephzibah High School in 1985. As a gifted student, she was assured scholarships to enter college. In 1985, she accepted an offer to attend North Carolina State University (NCSU) to major in pulp and paper science. "To be honest, I didn't know anything about the field when I arrived on the NCSU campus. However, I did know that the program was supporting me financially

while allowing me to accomplish my goal of obtaining an engineering degree."[1]

Once Chavonda found out what pulp and paper science was, she was only too eager to study it. She acquired amazing knowledge about using and replacing natural resources.

NCSU's College of Forest Resources, established in 1929, is one of the oldest schools of its type in the nation. Chavonda received a bachelor of science degree in pulp and paper science and technology in 1989. Realizing the many opportunities in this area, she continued her education, receiving a master of science degree in wood and paper science in 1992, and a Ph.D. in wood and paper science in 1998.

While pursuing her advanced degrees, Dr. Jacobs Young worked as a teacher's assistant at NCSU. By 1995, she was an acting professor at NCSU, teaching undergraduate and graduate courses in the paper science and engineering division of the College of Forest Resources. As a graduate student, Chavonda began conducting research on the use of biotechnology in the pulp and paper industry.

Dr. Jacobs Young has a strong belief in herself and never accepts the negative comments of others: "I remember once, while in graduate school, I was interested in applying for a very prestigious fellowship. I had a faculty member tell me that I didn't have any chance of receiv-

GIVING BACK

My mentors were all the strong African American role models I had in my life. My mother, while a working divorced mother of two daughters, who also financially supported her mother and sister, went to college and obtained a bachelor of science degree in nursing from the Medical College of Georgia. She enforced the need for us girls to have our own.[2]

—*Chavonda J. Jacobs Young*

DON'T BE AFRAID TO BE THE ONLY ONE

My advice to other females interested in science and math is to be persistent. Persistent in gathering information about their prospective field. Persistent in communicating with professionals in that field. I encourage them to have persistence to keep sight of the goal when it appears everyone and everything is working against you. They must also have persistence to break down barriers, not being afraid to be the *only* one. Don't ask why me . . . Say why *not* me![3]

—Chavonda J. Jacobs Young

ing it. That didn't stop me. I applied anyway. I didn't get the fellowship, but I received honorable mention and positive comments that helped me in successfully garnering other fellowships."[4]

On July 13, 1996, Chavonda married Arland Keith Young, an industrial engineer with the Boeing Company. They have a young daughter, Autumn Krystina.

Dr. Jacobs Young believes in shooting for the stars: "I believe that anything is possible. I am by no means done yet! There are so many things that I have yet to accomplish, including a master's degree in business. I have always felt that I am meant to do great things, but first I must be fully equipped. Education is the key!"[5]

Dr. Jacobs Young has held several positions in her field. She started as a chemist at E. I. DuPont de Nemours during the summer of 1988, but worked as an engineer the next summer. As a scientist at Kimberly-Clark Company, Dr. Jacobs Young researched how to increase the absorbency of disposable diapers. At Kraft General Foods, she analyzed the fiber in low-fat food. She has been widely published and has received numerous awards. Dr. Jacobs Young is currently an assistant professor in the College of Forest Resources, Division of Management and Engineering, at the University of Washington.

Chronology

1731	Benjamin Banneker born.
1776	Revolutionary War begins.
1783	Revolutionary War ends.
1790	First U.S. Patent Act enacted.
1806	Benjamin Banneker dies.
1849	Ellen F. Eglin born.
1850	Sara E. Goode born.
1861	Civil War begins.
1863	The Emancipation Proclamation is issued on January 1.
1864	Rebecca Lee Crumpler becomes the first African American woman to finish medical school, at the New England Female College.
1865	Civil War ends.
1867	Madame C. J. Walker born in Louisiana.
	Congress enacts a charter and designates Howard University as a "university for the education of youth in the liberal arts and sciences."
	Congress passes the first Reconstruction Act, requiring former Confederate states to ratify the Civil War amendments, write new constitutions, and grant voting rights to all males, regardless of "race, color, or previous condition of servitude."
	Congress passes the Thirteenth Amendment, abolishing slavery in the United States; it is later ratified.
1868	Howard University Medical School founded.
	Congress passes the Fourteenth Amendment, granting blacks full citizenship and equal rights; it is later ratified.
1869	Annie Turnbo Malone born in Metropolis, Illinois.
1870	Congress passes the Fifteenth Amendment, granting voting rights to all males.
1877	Reconstruction ends.
1881	Tuskegee Institute founded.
	Spelman College, the first college for black women in the United States, founded by Sophia B. Packard and Harriet E. Giles.
1883	Civil Rights Act overturned. The Supreme Court declares the Civil Rights Act of 1875 unconstitutional. The Court declares that the Fourteenth Amendment forbids states, but not citizens, from discriminating.

1884	Ida Wells, editor of *Free Speech,* a small newspaper in Memphis, carried out an investigation into lynching.
1885	Sarah E. Goode patents the cabinet-bed. She is believed to be the first African American woman to receive a patent for an invention (July 14, 1885).
1888	Miriam E. Benjamin patents the gong and signal chair for hotels (July 17, 1888).
1889	Roger Arliner Young born in Clifton Forge, Virginia.
1892	Sarah Boone patents her ironing board (April 16, 1892).
1896	Marjorie Stewart Joyner born in Monterey, Virginia.
	Archia L. Ross patents a runner for stoops.
	In the case of *Plessy vs. Ferguson,* the United States Supreme Court rules that "separate but equal" facilities for blacks are constitutional.
	Julia T. Hammonds invents an apparatus for holding yarn skeins, (December 15, 1896).
1900	The African American population of the United States is 8,833,994 (11.6 percent).
	Paris Exposition is held and the U.S. pavilion houses an exhibition on black Americans, including inventors.
1904	Daytona Literary and Industrial School for Training Negro Girls, now called Bethune Cookman College, founded by Mary McLeod Bethune in Daytona Beach, Florida.
1908	National Association for Colored Graduate Nurses founded.
1909	National Association for the Advancement of Colored People founded.
1910	Madame C. J. Walker moves her headquarters to Indianapolis, Indiana.
1911	The National Urban League begins.
1912	Madame C. J. Walker addresses the National Negro Business League.
1913	Henry E. Baker of the United States Patent Office publishes *The Colored Inventor* on the fiftieth anniversary of the Emancipation Proclamation.
	Bessie Blount Griffin born in Hickory, Virginia.
1917	United States enters World War I and 370,000 African Americans are in military service.
	Annie Turnbo Malone establishes Poro College in St. Louis, Missouri.
1919	Jane Cooke Wright born in New York City.
	Madame C. J. Walker dies.
	Congress passes the Nineteenth Amendment, granting women the right to vote.

This is the year of the "Red Summer," with twenty-six race riots between the months of April and October.

Alice H. Parker receives patent for heating furnace (December 23, 1919).

Dorothy Lavinia Brown, M.D., the first African American female surgeon, born in Philadelphia, Pennsylvania.

1920 Annie Turnbo Malone is a multimillionaire, worth more than $14 million.

Harlem Renaissance begins—a remarkable period of creativity for black writers, poets, and artists.

1921 Bessie Coleman becomes the first African American licensed pilot.

1924 Evelyn Boyd Granville born in Washington, D.C.

Jewel Plummer Cobb born in Chicago, Illinois.

1925 Angela D. Ferguson born in Washington, D.C.

1928 Marjorie Stewart Joyner receives a patent for the permanent-wave machine (November 17, 1928).

1929 Stock market crashes and the Great Depression begins.

1933 Ruth Ella Moore receives a Ph.D. in bacteriology from Ohio State University.

Willa Brown and Janet Waterford Bragg are the only female members of the first all–African American class at Curtiss-Wright Aeronautical School.

1935 Margaret Cheetham invents toy (April 16, 1935).

1938 Reatha Clark King born in Pavo, Georgia.

1939 World War II begins in Europe.

1940 Dr. Betty Wright Harris born in Louisiana.

1941 United States enters World War II.

Ruth Lloyd receives a Ph.D. in anatomy from Case Western University.

1942 Patricia Bath born in New York.

1943 Valerie Thomas born in Baltimore, Maryland.

1945 World War II ends.

1946 Shirley Ann Jackson born in Washington, D.C.

Frederick Douglass Patterson establishes the United Negro College Fund to help support black colleges and black students.

1947 National Medical Association founded.

1948 Marie Maynard Daly receives a Ph.D. in chemistry from Columbia University.

1949 Evelyn Boyd Granville receives a Ph.D. in mathematics from Yale University, becoming one of the first African Americans to receive this degree.

Marjorie Lee Browne receives a Ph.D. in mathematics from the University of Michigan.

1950 Lydia M. Holmes invents knockdown wheeled toy (November 14, 1950).

Alexa Canady born in Lansing, Michigan.

1951 Bessie Blount Griffin invents portable receptacle support (April 24, 1951).

1954 In the case of *Brown vs. Board of Education of Topeka,* the United States Supreme Court rules that "separate but equal" schools are unconstitutional and orders integration "with all deliberate speed."

1955 Doris Shockley becomes the first African American woman to earn a Ph.D. in pharmacology.

Elizabeth Lipford Kent receives a Ph.D. in nursing from the University of Michigan.

Rosa Parks refuses to give up her seat on a Montgomery, Alabama, bus to a white man, sparking the Civil Rights Movement.

Sharon J. Barnes born in Beaumont, Texas.

1956 Mary Beatrice Davidson Kenner receives patent for a healthcare device (May 15, 1956).

Mae Jemison born in Decatur, Alabama.

1957 Eighteen African Americans integrate Central High School in Little Rock, Arkansas.

1960 Iola O. Carter invents a nursery chair (February 9, 1960).

Four North Carolina A&T students sit in at a Woolworth lunch counter. They are refused service. Their demonstration sparks sit-ins across the South and eventually leads to other civil rights demonstrations.

1961 Charlayne Hunter-Gault is admitted to the University of Georgia.

James Meredith integrates the University of Mississippi.

Vivienne Malone-Mayes becomes the first African American faculty member at Baylor University.

1963 Aprille Joy Ericsson Jackson born in Brooklyn, New York.

1964 Roger Arliner Young dies.

1965 Martin Luther King, Jr., tells the March on Washington, "I have a dream . . . "

1967 Chavonda J. Jacobs Young born in Augusta, Georgia.

1969 Marie Van Brittan Brown receives patent for home security system utilizing television surveillance (December 2, 1969).

1973 Gertrude E. Downing receives a patent for her reciprocating corner and baseboard cleaning auxiliary attachment for rotary floor treatment machines (February 13, 1973).

Patricia Cowings receives Ph.D. in psychology from University of California at Davis.

1975   Virgie M. Ammons patents a fireplace damper actuating tool.

1976   Mary Beatrice Davidson Kenner receives patent for carrier attachment for invalid walkers (May 18, 1976).

1977   Reatha Clark King, Ph.D., becomes president of Metropolitan State University.

1979   Marjorie Lee Browne, Ph.D., dies.

1980   Shirley Mathis McBay becomes dean of students at the Massachusetts Institute of Technology.

Mildred Austin Smith receives patent for family relationships game (October 18, 1980).

Valerie Thomas receives patent for illusion transmitter (October 21, 1980).

1981   Jewel Plummer Cobb, Ph.D., becomes president of California State University in Fullerton.

Dale Emeagwali receives a Ph.D. from Georgetown University.

1984   Betty Harris, Ph.D., receives patent for her invention for a spot test for an explosive called triamino trinitrobenzene.

1986   Dr. Nira Sudarkasa selected president of Lincoln University.

1988   Reatha Clark King, Ph.D., becomes president of the General Mills Foundation.

Patricia Bath, M.D., receives patent for the laserphacoprobe (May 17, 1988).

1989   Marjorie Stewart Joyner receives award from the Patent Law Association of Chicago.

1990   Roselyn Epps, M.D., becomes the first African American president of the American Medicine Women's Association.

1991   Sharon Barnes receives patent for her invention of process and apparatus for contactless measurement of sample temperature (January 29, 1991).

1992   Mae Jemison, M.D., becomes the first African American woman astronaut to travel in space.

1993   Jocelyn Elders, M.D., sworn in as U.S. Surgeon General.

1995   Shirley Ann Jackson, Ph.D., becomes head of the Nuclear Regulatory Commission.

Patrice Francis Clark Washington becomes the first African American female pilot promoted to airline captain in aviation history.

1997   Patricia Cowings, Ph.D., receives patent for autogenic feedback training exercise system (December 9, 1997).

Only 4 of 927 electrical engineering doctoral degrees awarded to U.S. citizens were awarded to African American women.

Ursula M. Burns named a corporate officer at Xerox Corporation.

Ruane Sharon Jeter patents a handheld, multifunctional device in one housing including a stapler, staple remover, pencil sharpener, hole punch, calculator, tape measure, architectural and engineering scale.

1998   Patricia Bath, M.D., receives patent for the method and apparatus for ablating and removing cataract lenses (December 1, 1998).

1998   Aprille Joy Ericsson Jackson receives the 1998 NASA Goddard Honor Award.

2000   Ruth J. Simmons, former president of Smith College, elected as the eighteenth president of Brown University in Providence, Rhode Island.

NOTES

ELLEN F. EGLIN
1. *Woman Inventor Magazine,* April 1890.
2. Henry E. Baker. *The Colored Inventor: A Record of Fifty Years.* 1915. (Reprint New York: Arno Press, 1968).

SARAH E. GOODE
1. United States Patent and Trademark Office, Specifications forming part of Letters Patent Number 322,177, November 13, 1883, p. 1.

MIRIAM E. BENJAMIN
1. United States Patent and Trademark Office, Specifications forming part of Letters Patent Number 386,289, July 17, 1888, p. 1.
2. United States Patent and Trademark Office, Specifications forming part of Letters Patent Number 614,335, July 11, 1898, p. 1.

MADAME C. J. WALKER
1. Anne L. McDonald. *Women and Invention in America—Feminine Ingenuity* (New York: Ballantine Books, 1992), p. 299.
2. Ibid.

MARJORIE STEWART JOYNER, PH.D.
1. Christi Parker. "Sixty-three Years Later, Inventor Glad She Made Waves," *Chicago Tribune,* November 3, 1989, p. 4.
2. Ibid.
3. Ibid.
4. Ibid.
5. Ibid.

MARY BEATRICE DAVIDSON KENNER AND
MILDRED AUSTIN SMITH
1. United States Patent and Trademark Office, Specifications forming part of Letters Patent Number 4,354,643, November 18, 1980, p. 1.
2. United States Patent and Trademark Office, Specifications forming part of Letters Patent Number 4,230,321, May 10, 1979.

BESSIE BLOUNT GRIFFIN
1. United States Patent and Trademark Office, Specifications forming part of Letters Patent Number 2,550,554, April 24, 1951, p. 1.

EVELYN BOYD GRANVILLE, PH.D.
1. Author's interview with Evelyn Boyd Granville, Ph.D., November 12, 1999.
2. Ibid.
3. Ibid.

JEWEL PLUMMER COBB, PH.D.
1. Barbara Simmons, ed., and Brian Lanker, Photographer. *I Dream a World: Portraits of Black Women Who Changed America* (New York: Stewart, Tabori & Chang, 1989) p. 52.

REATHA CLARK KING, PH.D.

1. Reatha Clark King, *Reflections,* Metropolitan State University Foundation alumni publication, 1987, p. 2.
2. Ibid.
3. Ibid.

BETTY WRIGHT HARRIS, PH.D.

1. Author's interview with Betty Wright Harris, Ph.D., October 15, 1999.
2. Ibid.
3. United States Patent and Trademark Office, Specifications forming part of Letters Patent Number 4,618,452, October 21, 1986, p. 1.
4. Ibid, author's interview, October 15, 1999.

SHIRLEY ANN JACKSON, PH.D.

1. Shirley Ann Jackson, Ph.D. "Perpetuating a Tradition of Excellence." Acceptance speech for the presidency of Rensselaer Polytechnic Institute, December 11, 1998.
2. Ibid.

ALEXA CANADY, M.D.

1. Barbara Simmons, ed., and Brian Lanker, photographer. *I Dream a World: Portraits of Black Women Who Changed America* (New York: Stewart, Tabori & Chang, 1989), p. 128.
2. Patricia Anstett. "Neurosurgeon Finds the Joy in Healing: Young and Gifted, She Broke Barrier in Her Field," *The Detroit Free Press,* March 8, 1999, p. 1.

SHARON J. BARNES

1. Author's interview with Sharon J. Barnes, October 24, 1999.

MAE JEMISON, M.D.

1. Female Frontiers QuestChat Archive, National Aeronautics and Space Administration, March 3, 1999, p. 3.
2. Ibid.

APRILLE JOY ERICSSON JACKSON, PH.D.

1. Author's interview with Aprille Joy Ericsson Jackson, Ph.D., October 4, 1999.

DANNELLIA GLADDEN GREEN, PH.D.

1. Author's interview with Dannellia Gladden Green, Ph.D., October 15, 1999.
2. Ibid.
3. Ibid.
4. Ibid.
5. Ibid.

CHAVONDA J. JACOBS YOUNG, PH.D.

1. Author's interview with Chavonda J. Jacobs Young, Ph.D., November 5, 1999.
2. Ibid.
3. Ibid.
4. Ibid.
5. Ibid.

BIBLIOGRAPHY

Baker, Henry E. *The Colored Inventor: A Record of Fifty Years.* 1915. Reprint, New York: Arno Press, 1968.

Black Contributors to Science and Energy Technology. Washington, D.C.: Department of Energy, Office of Affairs, 1979.

Blashfield, Jean F. *Women Inventors: Sybilla Masters, Mary Beatrice Davidson Kenner, and Mildred Austin Smith, Stephanie Kwolek, Frances Gabe.* Capstone Press, 1996.

Brodie, James Michael. *Created Equal: The Lives and Ideas of Black American Inventors.* New York: William Morrow, 1993.

Carwell, Hattie. *Blacks in Science: Astrophysicist to Zoologist.* Smithtown, N.Y.: Exposition Press, 1977.

Haskins, James. *Outward Dreams: Black Inventors and Their Inventions.* New York: Bantam Books, 1991.

Hayden, Robert C. *Eleven African American Doctors.* New York: First Century Books, 1992.

Hill, Susan T. *Blacks in Undergraduate Science and Engineering Education.* Washington, D.C.: National Science Foundation, 1992.

Ives, Patricia Carter. "Patent and Trademark Innovations of Black Americans and Women," *Journal of the Patent Office Society* 62, No. 2, 1980.

James, Portia P. *The Real McCoy: African American Invention and Innovation, 1619–1930.* Washington, D.C.: Smithsonian Press, 1989.

Massey, Walter E. "A Success Story Amid Decades of Disappointment." *Science* 258: 1177–1179, November 13, 1992.

Matthews, Rose Christine. *Underrepresented Minorities and Women in Science, Mathematics and Engineering: Problems and Issues for the 1990's.* Washington, D.C.: Congressional Research Service, Library of Congress, 1990.

McDonald, Anne L. *Women and Invention in America.* New York: Ballantine Books, 1972.

McKissack, Patricia, and Fred McKissack. *African American Inventors.* Brookfield, Conn.: The Millbrook Press, 1994.

Piper, Edna Mary Aliyce, "Beyond the Next Veil: Black Women Inventors." UCLA dissertation, University Research Library, 1989.

Salzman, Jack, David Lionel Smith, and Cornel West, eds. *The Encyclopedia of African American Culture and History.* New York: Macmillan, 1996.

Sammons, Vivian O. *Blacks in Science and Medicine.* New York: Hemisphere Pub. Corp., 1990.

Simmons, Barbara, ed. and Brian Lanker, photographer. *I Dream a World: Portraits of Black Women Who Changed America.* New York: Stewart, Tabori & Chang, 1989.

Sluby, Patricia Carter. "Black Women and Inventors." *A Scholarly Journal of Black Women.* 6(2):34, Fall 1989.

Stone, Richard. "Industrial Efforts: Plenty of Jobs, Little Minority Support in Biotech." *Science* 262:1127, November 12, 1993.

Sullivan, Otha Richard. *African American Inventors.* New York: John Wiley & Sons, 1998.

White, Patricia E. *Women and Minorities in Science and Engineering: An Update.* Washington, D.C.: National Science Foundation, 1992.

Williams, Larry De Van. "Educating Minority Children in an Environment That Makes Engineering an Attainable Goal." *IEEE Communications Magazine* 28: 58–60, December 1990.

PICTURE CREDITS

Pages 8 and 14: courtesy of Photographs and Prints Div., Schomburg Center for Research in Black Culture, The New York Public Library/Astor, Lenox and Tilden Foundations; page 16: courtesy of the Library of Congress, Washington, D.C.; page 19: courtesy of Photographs and Prints Div., Schomburg Center for Research in Black Culture, The New York Public Library/Astor, Lenox and Tilden Foundations; page 20: courtesy of Moorland-Spingarn Research Center, Howard University, Washington, D.C.; page 22: courtesy of the Library of Congress, Washington, D.C.; page 28: courtesy of Photographs and Prints Div., Schomburg Center for Research in Black Culture, The New York Public Library/Astor, Lenox and Tilden Foundations; page 32: courtesy of Vivian B. Harsh Research Collection of Afro-American History and Literature, Chicago Public Library; page 36: portrait by Michelle Whelan; page 39: courtesy of Moorland-Spingarn Research Center, Howard University, Washington, D.C.; page 41: courtesy of the University of Illinois at Chicago; page 48: courtesy of Photographs and Prints Div., Schomburg Center for Research in Black Culture, The New York Public Library/Astor, Lenox and Tilden Foundations; page 50: courtesy of the Library of Congress, Washington, D.C.; page 52: courtesy of Photographs and Prints Div., Schomburg Center for Research in Black Culture, The New York Public Library/Astor, Lenox and Tilden Foundations; page 57: courtesy of California State University, Fullerton; page 73: courtesy of Moorland-Spingarn Research Center, Howard University, Washington, D.C.; page 78: photo by Shahar Azran; page 82: courtesy of Dr. Betty W. Harris; page 89: photo by Jeffrey John Fearing, Howard University; page 94: courtesy of NASA/MU-SPIN Project; page 96: courtesy of the Library of Congress, Washington, D.C.; page 98: courtesy of Rensselaer Polytechnic Institute; page 100: courtesy of Patricia Clark Kenschaft, Ph.D.; pages 103 and 107: courtesy of Alexa Canady, M.D.; page 105: A/P World Wide; page 109: courtesy of Sharon L. Barnes; page 113: courtesy of NASA; page 115: courtesy of NASA; page 118: courtesy of Ursula Burns; page 122: courtesy of Aprille Joy Jackson, Ph.D.; page 127: courtesy of Dannellia Gladden Green, Ph.D.; page 131: courtesy of Chavonda Jacobs-Young, Ph.D.

INDEX

psychiatrists, defined, 59
pulp and paper science, 132, 133

radiology, defined, 71
Reconstruction, 20
Reed, Judy W., 12
Rensselaer Polytechnic Institute, 101
resident doctors, defined, 59
Revolutionary War, 10
Rillieux, Norbert, 10

sample temperature, contactless measurement of 110
satellites, 95
schools, black, 18. *See also* colleges, historically black
schools, segregation in, 102, 104
security system, 96
Shockley, Doris, 92
sickle cell anemia, 74–75
skin cancer, 70, 71
slaves, as inventors, 1, 10, 15
smallpox remedy, 9
Smith, Mildred Austin, 47
Space Physics Analysis Network (SPAN), 95
space technology, 65, 81, 82, 95, 123–24. *See also* astronauts, African American women as
specimen, defined, 97
sugar refining engine, 10
Surgeon General, Elders as, 92
Tandy, Vertner, 29
teachers
  advice to, 67, 129
  African American, 18, 38, 39, 64, 66, 70–71, 100
technology, defined, 39
television surveillance system, 96

Telling Our Stories: Women in Science, 87
theoretical explanation, defined, 104
Thomas, Valerie, 93–95
tissue holder, 49
toymakers, 50
triamino trinitrobenzene (TATB), 86

United States Department of Energy, 86, 87
United States Patent and Trademark Office, 13, 15

voting rights, 18

Walker, Lelia, 25, 28, 30
Walker, Madame C. J., 25–30, 34, 40, 42, 43
Walker Manufacturing Company, 27–30, 42, 43
walkers, carrier attachment for, 49
weapons sites, cleanup of, 86, 87
Wells, Ida, 136
Whitney, Eli, 10
Woman Inventor, 7, 11
World War II, 51–53, 55
Wright, Jane Cooke, 56–61
Wright, Louis Tompkins, 56, 58, 59, 60

Xerox Corporation, 119–20

yarn holder, 17
Young, Chavonda J. Jacobs, 130–33
Young, James, 99
Young, Roger Arliner, 35–39

zoology, 35, 37–39, 71